Live Jesus!

Wisdom from Saints Francis de Sales and Jane de Chantal

Louise Perrotta, General Editor

theWORD
among us

The Word Among Us Press
9639 Doctor Perry Road
Ijamsville, Maryland 21754
ISBN: 0-932085-42-3

www.wau.org

Cover design by David Crosson
Wisdom Series Editor: Patricia Mitchell

Made and printed in the United States of America

Library of Congress Cataloging-in-Publication Data

Francis, de Sales, Saint, 1567-1622.
  [Selections. English. 2000]
  Live Jesus! : wisdom from saints Francis de Sales and Jane de Chantal/Louise
Perrotta, general editor.
          p.   cm.
  Includes bibliographical references (p.).
  ISBN 0-932085-42-3
          1.   Spiritual life—Catholic Church. I. Perrotta, Louise. II Chantal,
          Jeanne-Francoise de,
Saint, 1572-1641. Selections. English. 2000. III. Title

  BX2179.F8 L6513 2000
  248.4'82—dc21   00-040412

Table of Contents

Introduction

Compiling a short anthology can be a little like trying to bring someone just a small plate of treats from a buffet table that features a lavish array of gourmet foods and culinary triumphs. "How do I choose?" the awed diner wonders. "Everything looks so good!" And when it is a question of a spiritual feast prepared by two of the church's most skilled and insightful guides to holiness, the dilemma becomes acute indeed.

St. Francis de Sales—bishop, doctor of the church, patron of writers and journalists—and St. Jane de Chantal, his closest friend and coworker, have left a banquet for the soul that, although prepared in the seventeenth century, appeals to the needs and tastes of third-millennium Christians everywhere. In their writings you can find many of today's popular spiritual themes: simplicity of life; how to live serenely in a frenetic world; the importance of ordinary things; and finding your true focus. If you love Scripture, you will feel an affinity with the man whom St. Vincent de Paul once referred to as "a speaking gospel" and with the woman who knew her Bible well enough to count Old Testament figures like Abraham among her spiritual friends. Also appealing for us is Francis and Jane's discussion of deep spiritual matters in an accessible, easy tone of down-to-earth realism and practicality. Some have called this "inspired common sense."

Furthermore, although the two directed some writings to men and women living a consecrated religious life, others were aimed at helping ordinary lay people draw closer to God through their everyday circumstances. In an age that considered high sanctity attainable only within the cloister, this insistence on the real thing for people "in the world" was striking. Some 350 years later, in words that resonate with St. Francis' vision of the "true devotion" to which every Christian should aspire, the Second Vatican Council stated that "Christians in any state or walk of life are called to the fullness of Christian life and to the perfection of love" (*Lumen Gentium*, Dogmatic Constitution on the Church, 40). Wise and gentle advice on how to attain to this fullness and perfection is what you can expect as you turn to the words of St. Francis and St. Jane.

This book represents a tiny fraction of their writings, which, in the French originals, fill twenty-six volumes for him and eight for her. It draws from some newer translations, and also paraphrases and adapts from older ones. In this modest sampling you will find excerpts from:

—The *Introduction to the Devout Life:* Addressed to Philothea, meaning "she who loves God," this practical guide to virtue and holiness was written by Francis to meet the need for spiritual literature for men and women in ordinary family and work situations. First published in 1608 and reprinted up to forty times within the author's lifetime alone, this popular classic remains as relevant as ever today.

—The *Treatise on the Love of God:* Francis described this lofty, lengthy work as the "biography" of a little-known saint, Holy Charity. Written for Theotimus, "he who honors God," this profound and moving account of the love story between God and his people uses language reminiscent of the Song of Songs.

—*St. Francis de Sales: A Testimony*: This is the only piece of writing that St. Jane produced for public view. It is a legal document prepared in 1627 for the first official canonization inquiry into the sanctity of Francis de Sales, who had died five years before. "There has never been a better portrait than this," pronounced a famous literary critic of her day. Indeed, Jane's answers to the ecclesiastical court's fifty five questions bring St. Francis to life for us and testify to her own spiritual acuity and perception.

—*Spiritual conferences*: These consisted of talks given to the women of the Visitation of Holy Mary, the religious order cofounded by the two saints. Never actually written by Jane or Francis, these informal presentations were copied down as they were delivered or shortly afterward by some of the nuns who first heard them. Though addressed to women in religious life, the bulk of their advice on growing closer to God is useful for any disciple of Christ.

—*Letters of spiritual direction*: These empathetic, tailor-made responses to the individual needs of their correspondents—some "in religion," some "in the world"—are especially revealing of Jane's and Francis' personalities and styles of guiding people to God. Just over two thousand letters survive from each saint.

Obviously, with such abundance to choose from, a book the size of this one can function only like that small plate at the banquet. We hope it whets your appetite for more (some suggestions for further reading appear in the Sources and Acknowledgments section on page 139). We also hope that *Live Jesus! Wisdom from Saints Francis de Sales and Jane de Chantal* will serve you as an aid to prayer and an encouragement to deeper intimacy with God—that loving union of hearts to which Jesus calls each of us. Finally, may your reading help you to approach Francis and Jane as two new friends who stand ready to help you toward this goal and whose tested wisdom has already yielded the fruits of holiness in many lives.

Louise Perrotta
General Editor

1

Friends on the Road to Holiness:

THE LIVES OF FRANCIS DE SALES AND JANE DE CHANTAL

Not every Catholic shouted glad hosannas when Francis de Sales was canonized in 1665, forty-three years after his death. The path leading to God described by de Sales and his coworker, Jane Frances de Chantal, was "too easy," some grumbled. It had been made "a pleasant road," wrote one commentator derisively.

Of course, the majority opinion about Francis and Jane was overwhelmingly positive. Still, the criticism underscores the fact that most seventeenth-century Catholics found it somewhat shocking to think that people in all walks of life—and not just priests and nuns—were called to holiness. Yet Jane and Francis had learned from personal experience that a lay person busy with work, studies, family, and friends could cultivate a deep relationship with God, not *despite* but *through* these ordinary life circumstances. Francis, after all, had lived almost half his life by the time he was ordained a priest; Jane was thirty-eight when she entered religious life.

Rooted in the Real World

The world into which Francis and Jane were born—in 1567 and 1572, respectively—was wracked by political and religious warfare, pulsing with new ideas, and undergoing spiritual renewal. A Catholic revival was underway as the church corrected the abuses that had spawned the Protestant reformation. Missionary zeal was reawakened, spiritual writings were in demand, and religious orders were being created or energized.

Both Jane and Francis were born into strong Catholic families. He was the eldest of eight surviving children of aristocratic parents living in Savoy, an independent duchy that spanned the Alps. Jane's birthplace was Dijon, a wealthy city in central France. The second of three children of a prominent lawyer, Jane never really knew her mother, who died in childbirth, or her stepmother, who died while Jane was a toddler.

Jane's education, designed to equip her for marriage into a noble family, was far broader than that usually offered to girls, and included a sound, practical formation in faith, current events, and financial and legal affairs. All of this she put to good use when, at twenty, she married Baron Christophe de Rabutin-Chantal and took over managing the estates he had neglected while away on military campaigns.

Openhearted Dedication to God's People

Earlier that same year, in 1592, Francis was admitted to the bar at Chambéry, the capital of Savoy. This marked the culmination of years of study: ten in Paris, where Francis acquired the typical nobleman's knowledge of the humanities, philosophy, and social arts; then three more in Padua, Italy, studying law.

Francis, however, had never desired the court career for which his legal training had prepared him. From an early age, he had known that he was called by the Lord to become a priest, and also that his father would object. As Francis later explained, he had only studied law "to please my father," while he had secretly pursued theology "to please myself."

Finally, he was offered gifts he could not accept—an estate and a title, an arranged marriage, and a prestigious appointment to the Savoy Senate. Francis declared his true desires. Through an unexpected act of providence—an invitation to assume the diocese's second most important post under the bishop of Geneva—he received his father's grudging approval to pursue his priestly vocation.

Ordained later that year, Francis soon volunteered for a dangerous mission to the Chablais, a region on the south bank of Lake Geneva. His assignment: to bring to Catholicism the area's twenty-five thousand inhabitants, most of whom had become Calvinists when the Swiss had invaded the area sixty years earlier. Undeterred by public indifference or hostility, illness, severe weather, hired assassins, and even a pack of hungry wolves, Francis kept at his task for four years. He preached, distributed pamphlets, celebrated Mass, and initiated friendly theological discussions with individual Protestant leaders. Eventually, drawn by his personal holiness and gentle persuasion, almost all the people of the Chablais became Catholic.

In 1602, Francis was named bishop of Geneva. It was not a position he had sought. "If it comes to me, it will have to be borne," he wrote a friend. "If not, I shall feel so much better."

Any reluctance Francis may have felt left him once he moved into the modest bishop's house in the mountain town of Annecy. From this makeshift see (Geneva, the diocese's official center, was under Calvinist control), he began shepherding his diocese with single-minded dedication.

For the next twenty years, Francis devoted himself to implementing church reforms and encouraging personal renewal. He made preaching a priority ("a bishop's first duty," he called it) and addressed kings and peasants alike with a simple eloquence that moved hearts. He taught catechism classes for children. He made badly needed changes in the way priests were selected and trained, personally examining each candidate, and ordained a total of nine hundred men.

Despite his official and administrative responsibilities, this bishop was always accessible. "He never turned anyone away . . . nor did he show any signs of weariness or aversion," Jane de Chantal would later write of him. Francis spent long hours in the confessional, welcoming especially the penitents other confessors might turn away because they were "wretched," "diseased," or "foul-smelling." Through personal meetings and scores of letters of spiritual direction—some twenty to thirty each day—he led many individuals closer to Christ. The same pastoral aim inspired him to write two books for which he would become famous—*Introduction to the Devout Life* and *Treatise on the Love of God*—works that even today continue to point the way to intimacy with God.

A Reversal and a Redirection

As Francis' call to serve the church unfolded, Jane was energetically pursuing her own vocation a few hundred miles to the north.

She and Christophe were happily married, devoted to one another and to their four children. A sociable pair, they had many friends and entertained freely when the baron was at home. This happy round of activities came to a sudden end in October 1601, when Christophe was mortally wounded in a hunting accident. He lay dying for nine days, a model of Christian resignation and forgiveness toward the friend who had shot him.

Jane, on the other hand, was wild with grief. At first she denied the obvious and then she bargained desperately with God: "Take everything I have, my relatives, my belongings, my children, but leave me my husband!" After Christophe's death, it would be years before she could fully forgive his unfortunate hunting partner.

Jane's anguish became a bridge to deeper union with God. As she struggled to accept her loss, the twenty-eight-year-old widow experienced an intense desire to love the Lord with wholehearted dedication, as she had loved Christophe. She made a vow never to remarry. She gave away her jewels and greatly simplified her lifestyle. She adopted a rule of life that gave all her time to prayer, works of mercy, and the care and teaching of her children. She found a confessor—not the most skilled spiritual director, as it turned out—who unwisely increased her penitential practices. He made her vow, among other things, never to reveal anything he said or to consult anyone but him about her spiritual life.

In Jane's world, a young widow with four young children had few options. When, therefore, Christophe's father threatened to disinherit the children unless the family came to live with him, Jane acquiesced. As she soon discovered, the old man lived with his five illegitimate children and their mother, a scheming housekeeper who treated Jane with contempt. Jane bore this treatment for seven years, learning to respond to insults with love and humility and distinguishing herself, too, by caring for the sick in a hospital-dispensary she set up in the attic.

A Friendship Unfolds

In March 1604, Bishop Francis de Sales came to Dijon to give a series of Lenten sermons in one of the local churches. Jane de Chantal installed herself right up front near the pulpit. The bishop recognized her immediately. She was the woman he had once seen in a vision, whom God had revealed as his future coworker in the founding of a religious congregation.

For her part, Jane saw in Francis the priest she had seen in a vision that had flooded her soul with joy and trust soon after Christophe's death. "This is the man beloved of God and among men into whose hands you are to commit your conscience," an inner voice had told her.

Jane was experiencing a crisis of faith at the time and longed to consult Francis. In spite of the vow of fidelity she had made to her spiritual director, she asked Bishop de Sales for a private meeting.

Francis understood her predicament. During his student years, he had gone through periods of near despair at the thought that he might be eternally damned. Only by entrusting himself to God's mercy and focusing on the present moment had he found relief. "Whatever happens, Lord, may I at least love you in this life if I cannot love you in eternity," Francis wrote at the height of his suffering.

Francis urged Jane to similar acceptance of her spiritual state and advised her to counter temptations with absolute trust in God's mercy. Doubts against the faith, as well as spiritual dryness, would test Jane for the rest of her life, but Francis' strategy enabled her to overcome them with joyful serenity. In fact, Vincent de Paul, who guided Jane for the last twenty years of her life, testified that faith was her chief virtue.

It must have been a profound relief to Jane when, four months after their first talk, the bishop became her spiritual director. Francis, for his part, was convinced that this friendship was part of God's divine plan. "God gave me to you," he assured Jane in the first of many letters.

Birth of a Religious Community

Jane spent the next few years learning to curb what Francis identified as an overanxious, "straining eagerness" for spiritual perfection. His motto was: "Everything with love, nothing by force." She had worried that she might be disobeying God by remaining with her children instead of entering a convent. On the contrary, said Francis. While he was sure that the religious life was in Jane's future, in the meantime she was right to follow her motherly instincts. Jane's path to holiness lay in embracing her current state and duties.

In June 1607, Francis shared with Jane an idea for a new type of religious community that would dispense with the customary age and health restrictions. Open to any woman who felt drawn to deeper devotion, this congregation would be both "active" and "contemplative"—centered on prayer, but including outreach to the sick and poor.

Four months later, a tragic death set in motion the chain of events that made Francis' idea a reality. His beloved youngest sister, fifteen-year-old Jeanne, fell ill and died of fever and dysentery while visiting Jane and her family. Grief-stricken and feeling responsible for the girl's death, Jane vowed to make it up to the de Sales family by championing an idea that Francis' mother had already proposed: a marriage between Jane's oldest daughter, Marie-Aimée, and the youngest de Sales son, Bernard. Everyone was in favor of the match, including the prospective bride and groom.

The wedding, which took place in 1610, made it reasonable for Jane to move to Annecy and begin the foundation of what would become the Visitation Order. In Annecy, Jane would be close to the young bride and able to help her learn the art of managing an estate. Françoise, Jane's second daughter, would live with her in the convent. Charlotte, her youngest, was also going to live in the convent, but she died unexpectedly of a fever just before the move. As for Jane's only son, fifteen-year-old Celse-Bénigne, he was already living with her father in Dijon and would soon leave for Paris.

The fact that Jane loved her children deeply and provided for them carefully tends to be obscured by an ugly incident that marred her final good-byes at the Dijon family home. As Jane moved toward the door, Celse-Bénigne surprised everyone by melodramatically throwing himself across the threshold. "I'm not strong enough to hold you back," he cried out, "but at least people will say that you trampled your own child underfoot!"

Years later, after Jane succeeded in arranging a good match for him, Celse-Bénigne wrote to express his delight and to apologize for his youthful behavior. But right up until his death in battle in 1627, this headstrong son gave his mother constant anxiety by his gambling, duelling, and general instability.

Busy Years of Growth and Grace

Jane and three other women moved into their Annecy quarters on Trinity Sunday, 1610, and took up a simple routine of prayer, work, recreation, and silence. Despite their different backgrounds, these Visitation pioneers experienced a season of special grace. God gave them "such great love," wrote Jane, that their life together was truly "a paradise."

Francis gave the women informal teachings, served as unofficial novice-master, and supported Jane with advice and encouragement. As superior of the budding community, Jane developed a firm but tenderly maternal approach that allowed Francis's vision for religious life to become a reality.

Women were drawn to the group, and it grew quickly. By 1615 Jane was traveling to Lyons to establish the first Visitation house in France. It was the first of many new houses (eighty by the time of Jane's death) and the first of the many arduous journeys that would characterize the rest of her life—no small sacrifice for a woman who once confided that she disliked great activity.

Francis, too, longed for tranquility, especially as the years passed and diocesan affairs became more burdensome. "This is where I will retire!" he exclaimed while visiting a mountain hermitage in 1621. Here the overworked bishop could imagine himself with ample time for prayer and for the many writing projects he still had in mind.

But this was not to be. Exhausted by the unsparing pace at which he had served his people, Francis suffered a stroke on December 27 of the following year. He died the next day, at the age of fifty-five, after patiently enduring the application of a red-hot poker to his temples—one of the "extreme measures" prescribed by contemporary medical science.

God Alone

"He is no longer alive," an interior voice alerted Jane on December 28, during a visit to a foundation in Grenoble, France. Reluctant to take the message at face value, Jane interpreted it to mean that Francis had become so lost in Christ that, like St. Paul, he could now say, "It is no longer I who live, but Christ, who lives in me" (Galatians 2:20). Only after Epiphany did she learn the truth.

"I wept a great deal all the rest of that day and the whole night until after Holy Communion," Jane wrote to one of the nuns. And to her brother: "My soul is filled with grief." At the same time, she assured him, it is "also full of the peace of God's will."

In fact, God had been preparing Jane over the last several years to accept this sacrifice. Four years before, she had sensed that God was calling her to become more detached from Francis. Francis had confirmed this sense in words that Jane carried in her pocket until the day she died: "Our Lord loves you, my dear mother, he wants you to be all his. Let no other arm carry you now; his providence alone shall be your rest. Do not look elsewhere."

In the years that followed, Francis and Jane communicated frequently by mail but saw one another less and less, as their particular duties called them to travel different ways. Their last meeting took place in Lyons a few weeks before Francis died. It was their first encounter in three years, and they spent it discussing matters related to the order.

The remaining twenty years of Jane's life brought ample opportunity for increased reliance on God. By the time she died of pneumonia on December 13, 1641, at the age of sixty-nine, she had outlived her closest companions in religious life as well as all but one of her children. Undeterred, she devoted herself to instilling Francis' spirit in the order they had founded and spent her days in a whirlwind of travel, letter-writing, teaching, and administration. To her great embarrassment, Jane became known far and wide for her sanctity. Her joyful, motherly love invited openness, and many lay people sought her out for spiritual help.

What attracted people to Jane and Francis in their own lifetimes is, in many ways, what continues to attract us today. It is a word of hope—the assurance that God loves us and wants to meet us in the ordinary circumstances of our lives. Father Joseph F. Power of the Oblates of St. Francis de Sales, a religious order inspired by the teachings of the saint, has written: "In many ways Salesian spirituality is one of Jesus coming to our homes—to where we live, work, play, and pray." And as Jesus dwells in our hearts, we are able "to 'find' him wherever we are, in what we do, and in the relationships that form our lives."

2

God Is Calling

RESTLESS TILL WE REST IN GOD

We have a natural tendency towards absolute goodness. Because of this, our heart is touched with a certain anxious desire and continual uneasiness. We cannot quiet ourselves, or stop desiring that perfect satisfaction and utter contentment. But when, through faith, our hearts perceive this lovely object that we so naturally desire—Oh! Theotimus, what joy! What pleasure! How our whole soul is thrilled. So amazed at the sight of such unsurpassed beauty, we cry out with love: "Behold, you are beautiful, my love; behold you are beautiful" (Song of Songs 1:15). . . .

By a deep and secret instinct, in all that we do, we desire and look for happiness. We grope around and seek it here and there, without knowing where it is or what it is made of. Then faith opens our eyes, and we see the infinite wonders of God. Having found the treasure we sought—Oh! What a satisfaction to our poor human heart! What joy, what loving contentment! "Oh, I have met with him, whom my heart sought without knowing him! O how little I knew what I was searching for, when nothing made me content in all that I found, because, in fact, I did not know what I was looking for. I was seeking to love and did not know what to love. Therefore, not finding my true love, my love remained as a true but unrecognized desire. I had indeed enough foretaste of love to make me seek it, but not enough knowledge of the goodness I had to love, to actually be able to love." ❧

St. Francis de Sales
Treatise on the Love of God

NOW IS THE ACCEPTABLE TIME

God is so good that he never ceases to work in our hearts to draw us out of ourselves, out of vain and perishable things, so that we can receive his grace and give ourselves wholly to him. One person he calls by a sermon, another by an example, this one by some holy reading or by his inspiration alone, others by certain afflictions. In fact, he gives his grace to each sufficiently and abundantly for salvation, and for growing and maturing in our faith. . . .

Grace never fails us, never leaves us, unless we leave it. Our good God waits for us patiently in our delays, he unceasingly calls us even though we don't answer him; he knocks at the very door of the heart which is shut to him. . . .

When we feel urged to depart from a sin, to leave an imperfection, to correct a negligence, to grow in virtue, to make rapid strides to the perfection of divine love, then, the hour is come for us. Let us arise in haste, let us run to the divine Spouse, accept his grace, benefit by his inspiration; it is the hour of our deliverance (cf. 2 Corinthians 6:2); let us not delay, let us run. . . .

There occurs to me on this subject a somewhat amusing comparison. I remember that Monsieur de Chantal was very fond of lying in bed in the morning. I had to rise early, since I had to look after the affairs of the house. . . . When it began to be late and I had gone back to the bedroom, making noise enough to awaken him, so that Mass might be said in the chapel and afterwards the remaining affairs might be seen to, I would become impatient. I would go and draw the bed curtains and call to him that it was late, that he must get up, that the chaplain was vested and was going to begin Mass. Finally I used to take a lighted taper and hold it before his eyes and torment him so much that at last I would awaken him and make him get out of bed.

What I mean to tell you by this little story is that our Lord does the same with us. After having long and patiently waited for us, and seeing that we are not correcting our faults through the ordinary means, he comes nearer to us, draws the curtain of certain difficulties himself, brings his light right up to our eyes, entreats and urges us so strongly that often he forces us, as if by gentle violence, to arise. And when we feel his touch, and have his light, we must obey him, and rise quickly. . . .

When by our negligence we stop benefiting from these precious inspirations sent by the Lord, we may rightly fear that the favorable time will not return for us. The same Lord has said: "A time shall come that you shall seek me and shall not find me; you shall call and I will not answer you" (cf. Proverbs 1:28). . . .

Respond to the Lord's attractions whatever it costs you. Heaven suffers violence, and the violent bear it away (Matthew 11:12). We must conquer and overcome ourselves valiantly and follow God when he calls us—faithfully and humbly, working out the work of our salvation with fear and trembling, because the way that leads to life is so narrow that few enter it (cf. Philippians 2:12; Matthew 7:14). ◆

> St. Jane de Chantal
> *Her Exhortations,*
> *Conferences and Instructions*

THINK OF CHRIST, WHO ALWAYS THINKS OF YOU

Be conscious of the love with which Jesus Christ our Lord suffered so much in this world, especially in the Garden of Olives and on Mount Calvary. You were the object of this love. By means of all these sufferings, he obtained from God the Father good resolutions and decisions for your heart. By the same means he obtained also all that you need to observe, nurture, strengthen and carry out these resolutions. Firm resolutions, how precious you are, being the child of such a mother as is the Passion of my Savior! How much should I cherish you, since you have been so dear to my Jesus. My Savior, you died to win for me the grace to make my deliberate decisions. Grant me the grace to die rather than forsake them.

Remember, Philothea, the heart of our Lord saw your heart, and loved you surely from the tree of the cross. By this love he obtained for you all the good things that you will ever have, including your resolutions. Yes, Philothea, we can say with Jeremiah: "Lord, before I existed you beheld me and called me by name" (cf. 1:5). This is indeed so; his divine goodness has prepared in his love and mercy all the means, general and particular for our salvation, and consequently our resolutions. Yes, without doubt. A woman with child prepares the cradle, the linen and swaddling clothes, and even arranges a nurse for the child whom she hopes to bring forth, though it is not yet in the world. So our Lord, his goodness, as it were pregnant with you, wishing to bring you forth to salvation and make you his child, prepared upon the tree of the cross everything you would need. He got ready your spiritual cradle, linen, and swaddling clothes, your nurse and everything suitable for your happiness. These are all the means, all the attractions and all the graces by which he guides you and wants to lead you to perfection.

My God, how deeply this truth should be fixed in our memory. Is it possible that I have been loved, and loved so tenderly, by my Savior? That he thought of me personally in all these little events by which he has drawn me to himself? How much then should we love, cherish and make good use of all this for our benefit! This is extremely kind: this loving heart of my God thought of Philothea, loved her and obtained for her a thousand means of salvation. This he did as though there was no other soul in the world he could think of. The sun shines on one part of the earth, shining on it no less than if it shone nowhere else, and as if it shone upon it alone. In the same way, our Lord thought of and cared for all his loving children in such a way that he thought of each one of us as though he had not thought of all the rest. He loved me, says St. Paul, and gave himself for me (Galatians 2:20); as if he said: for myself alone, as though he had done nothing for the others. Imprint this in your spirit, Philothea, in order to cherish and nourish with care your firm resolution so precious to the heart of the Savior.

St. Francis de Sales
Introduction to the Devout Life

HOW TO RESPOND TO GOD DAY BY DAY

From a letter to her brother André Frémyot, Archbishop of Bourges:

Since God, in his eternal goodness, has moved you to consecrate all your love, your actions, your works, and your whole self to him utterly without any self-interest but only for his greater glory and his satisfaction, remain firm in this resolve. With the confidence of a son, rest in the care and love which divine providence has for you in all your needs. Look upon providence as a child does its mother who loves him tenderly. You can be sure that God loves you incomparably more. We can't imagine how great is the love which God, in his goodness, has for souls who thus abandon themselves to his mercy, and who have no other wish than to do what they think pleases him, leaving everything that concerns them to his care in time and in eternity.

After this, every day in your morning exercise, or at the end of it, confirm your resolutions and unite your will with God's in all that you will do that day and in whatever he sends you. Use words like these: "O most holy will of God, I give you infinite thanks for the mercy with which you have surrounded me; with all my strength and love, I adore you from the depths of my soul and unite my will to yours now and forever, especially in all that I shall do and all that you will be pleased to send me this day, consecrating to your glory my soul, my mind, my body, all my thoughts, words and actions, and my whole being. I beg you, with all the humility of my heart, accomplish in me your eternal designs, and do not allow me to present any obstacle to this. Your eyes, which can see the most intimate recesses of my heart, know the intensity of my desire to live out your holy will, but they can also see my weakness and limitations. That is why, prostrate before your infinite mercy, I implore you, my Savior, through the gentleness and justice of this same will of yours, to grant me the grace of accomplishing it perfectly, so that, consumed in the fire of your love, I may be an acceptable holocaust which, with the glorious Virgin and all the saints, will praise and bless you forever. Amen."

During the activities of the day, spiritual as well as temporal, as often as you can, . . . unite your will to God's by confirming your morning resolution. Do this either by a simple, loving glance at God, or by a few words spoken quietly and cast into his heart, by assenting in words like: "Yes, Lord, I want to do this action because you want it," or simply, "Yes, Father," or, "O Holy Will, live and rule in me," or other words that the Holy Spirit will suggest to you. You may also make a simple sign of the cross over your heart, or kiss the cross you are wearing. All this will show that above everything, you want to do the holy will of God and seek nothing but his glory in all that you do.

St. Jane de Chantal
Letters of Spiritual Direction

3

A Simple Focus

KEEP YOUR EYES ON GOD

Do as little children who with one hand hold fast to the hand of their father and with the other gather strawberries or blackberries along the hedges. In the same manner, while gathering and managing the goods of this world with one hand, hold fast with the other to the hand of your heavenly Father, turning to him from time to time to see if your actions or occupations are pleasing to him. Take care, above all, that you do not leave his hand and protection thinking of collecting and gathering more. For if he abandons you, you would not take even a single step without falling flat on your face to the ground. I mean, Philothea, that amidst your ordinary affairs and occupations which do not require a strict and earnest attention, you [should] look more at God than at your affairs. When matters of great importance are at hand that require all your attention to do them well, you [should] look at God from time to time, as sailors do, who, in order to reach the land they desire, look more at the sky above than on the ocean below where they sail. Thus God will work with you, in you and for you, and your work will be followed by consolation. ❧

St. Francis de Sales
Introduction to the Devout Life

WALK SIMPLY AND WITH CONFIDENCE

Don't examine so anxiously whether you're being perfect or not. . . . This self-examination, when it is made with anxiety and perplexity, is just a waste of time. Those who engage in it are like soldiers who, in training for combat, have so many mock battles and drills among themselves that when it comes right down to the real thing, they find themselves tired and spent. Or they are like musicians who get hoarse with practicing to sing a motet. The mind wearies itself with such a searching and continual examination, and when it comes to the moment of action it can do no more. . . .

"If your eye is simple, your whole body will be full of light," says our Savior (Matthew 6:22). Simplify your judgment; don't reflect and dwell so much on yourself, but walk simply and with confidence. For you, there are only God and yourself in this world; all the rest should not touch you, except insofar as God commands and in the way he commands. I beg you, don't look about you so much; keep your gaze fixed on the relationship between God and yourself. . . . Don't look—I mean, with a fixed, deliberate gaze—at anything except this; just glance at all the rest.

Therefore, don't examine what others are doing or speculate about what will happen to them, but regard them with a simple, kind, gentle, and affectionate eye. ❧

St. Francis de Sales
Letters to Persons in Religion

ONLY ONE THING IS NECESSARY

Do not examine yourself in order to learn if you are to persevere, if you are being faithful, if you are pleasing to God. Empty yourself of your very self and of every anxiety, apprehension, trouble, or fear. . . . Your remedy will be a simple gazing upon God, with no attempt to reply to him. Once more, in God's name I tell you this. You look into yourself far too much. Do not any longer find cause for trouble in your trouble. . . .

Hold your eyes on God and *leave the doing to him*. That is all the *doing* you have to worry about, and the only activity which God asks of you and towards which it is he alone who is drawing you.

I may add that it is this that our blessed father [Francis de Sales] would always order me to practice, holding the mind in all simplicity and directness, without act or effort, in that simple gaze upon God and contemplation of God, in total surrender to his will; without a wish to see, or feel, or carry out any work, but merely content to remain in his presence—relaxed, at peace, confident, patient, never inspecting self to see how things are going, nor what one is doing, feeling, or enduring. No, you must not inquire what your soul is doing, has done, or will do, nor what may happen to it in any future event or contingency. From this position you must not budge because this sole and single gaze upon God embraces all our duty, especially in a state of suffering. . . . *One thing alone is necessary:* it is to have God. In short, then, no matter what is going on, we must hold both our attention and our love on God, not wasting our time in studying what is happening to ourselves, nor what is its cause. Our Lord asks this of us.

St. Jane de Chantal
St. Chantal on Prayer

SIMPLE SELF-FORGETFULNESS LEADS TO PEACE

The mark of our fidelity is when we are entirely abandoned to God, when we wish for God only, when we are satisfied with him. . . . But we want and seek so many things along with God that this hinders us from finding him. We want to be loved and highly regarded and we think that everything we do should be approved of. . . . This only serves to make us restless and troubled. If we sought God only, we would always be content and would find all things in him.

Yes, a soul may indeed be tranquil amid its trials. . . . We see some people who suffer greatly and who are at the same time extremely gentle and sweet in their conversation. This comes from their having made their will die in God's will. But people who are keenly sensitive to some small thing, certainly, have not tried to subordinate their wills to God's. What is the remedy for this? We must keep ourselves in God's presence and look at him near us. . . . In order not to lose interior peace, we must do what our blessed father [Francis de Sales] says: *Go to God without reflecting on what pains us.* . . .

This is what you must do. Suppose you have a little pain in your head or stomach, or you've made a great blunder, or you've been upset. Don't stop at all that. Pass on and go to God without scrutinizing your trouble. "But I want to look at it so I can offer it to God." That's good. But when you offer it to him, don't look on your trouble so much that you magnify it and confirm that you have good reason to complain. Oh, indeed, we must be more courageous and abandon ourselves totally to God, wishing for him only and being satisfied with him alone.

How lovely simplicity is! ⚬

> St. Jane de Chantal
> *Her Exhortations,*
> *Conferences and Instructions*

WHEN TEMPTATIONS DISTRACT

From a letter to Jane de Chantal:

Your temptations against faith have come back, and although you don't answer them even a word, they press you. You don't argue with them: that's good, my child. But you think too much of them; you fear them too much; you dread them too much. Otherwise, they wouldn't do you any harm. You are too sensitive to temptations. You love the faith and don't want to have a single thought come to you that is contrary to faith. As soon as a single one arises, you grieve about it and distress yourself. You're too jealous of this purity of faith; everything seems to spoil it. No, no, my child, let the wind blow, and don't take the rustling of the leaves for the clashing of arms.

Lately I was near the beehives, and some of the bees flew onto my face. I wanted to raise my hand and brush them off. "No," a peasant said to me. "Don't be afraid and don't touch them. They won't sting you at all unless you touch them." I trusted him, and not one stung me. Trust me: don't fear these temptations; don't touch them, and they won't hurt you. Pass on and don't spend time with them. . . .

Be quite convinced that all the temptations of hell can't possibly stain a soul that doesn't love them: let them have their course then. The Apostle St. Paul suffered terrible temptations, and God didn't will to take them away from him—and all out of love!

Come, come, my child, courage. Let your heart be ever with its Jesus, and let this vile beast bark at the gate as much as he likes. . . . In the end, God will raise you up and cause you to rejoice and "will make you see the desire of your heart" (cf. Psalm 20:4). ∽

St. Francis de Sales
Letters to Persons in the World

LOVING GOD FOR HIMSELF

It is difficult, I confess, to take delight in the beauty of a mirror without catching sight of ourselves and liking that. Yet there is a difference between the pleasure we take in enjoying the beauty of the mirror, and the self-satisfaction we take in seeing ourselves in it. It is also without doubt very hard to love God and not also love the pleasure which we take in his love, yet there is a difference between the pleasure we take in loving God because he is beautiful, and the joy we take in loving him because his love gives us pleasure. Now our task must be to seek in God only the love of his beauty, not the pleasure which is in the beauty of his love.

At prayer, if you notice that you are praying, you are diverting your attention from God to whom you pray, and giving it to the prayer by which you pray. The anxious concern we have not to be distracted often causes us the greatest distraction! Simplicity is the best way in spiritual things. If you wish to contemplate God, contemplate him then, with all your attention. If you start to look back on yourself, to see how you look when you look upon him, it is not God you look at but yourself. Those who pray fervently do not know whether they pray or not, for they are not thinking of the prayer they make but of God to whom they make it. He who is in the fire of sacred love does not turn his heart back upon himself to see what he is doing, but keeps it focused upon God whom he loves. . . .

Look at that man over there who prays, apparently with great devotion and with ardent love. But stay a little, and you will discover whether it is God whom he loves. As soon as the delight and satisfaction which he took in love departs, and dryness comes, he will stop short, and only casually pray. If it had been God whom he loved, why would he stop loving him, since he is always God? It was the consolations of God that he loved, not the God of consolation.

There are many people who take no delight in divine love unless it is sugar-coated, and they act like children who, if they have a little honey spread on their bread, lick off the honey and throw away the bread. So when they follow love for the sake of its sweetness and do not find the sweetness, they disregard the love. For them, the danger lies in either turning back as soon as they miss their consolations, or in spending time in vain sweetness, which is far from true love.

St. Francis de Sales
Treatise on the Love of God

How to Keep Your Focus

You tell me that you do not have the time to give two or three hours to prayer; who asks you to do so? Recommend yourself to God the first thing in the morning, protest that you do not wish to offend him, and then go about your affairs, resolved, nevertheless, to raise your spirit to God, even amidst company. Who can prevent you from speaking to him in the depth of your heart, since it makes no difference whether you speak to him mentally or vocally? . . .

St. Jerome relates that when someone went to visit [the holy fathers who lived in the desert], they heard one of the fathers saying, "You, O my God, are all that I desire"; and another father: "When shall I be all yours, O my God"; and another repeating: "Deign, O God, to rescue me" (cf. Psalm 70:1). . . .

The [Divine] Spouse says in the Song of Songs that his beloved has ravished his heart with one glance of her eyes (4:9). . . . These words are a quiver full of most agreeable and most delightful interpretations. Here is one which is very pleasing: when a husband and wife have household matters which compel them to be separated, if it happens by chance that they meet, they glance at one another as they pass. . . . In like manner this Spouse wishes to say: Although my beloved may be very much occupied, nevertheless she does not fail to look at me with one eye, assuring me by this glance that she is all mine. She has ravished my heart . . . with one thought which comes from her heart. ❧

> St. Francis de Sales
> *Sermons on Prayer*

SINGLE-MINDED LOVE OF GOD

From Jane de Chantal's testimony for the canonization process of Francis de Sales:

I t is my certain belief that our blessed founder's life was an uninterrupted prayer because he had only a single aim in all he did. . . . I can affirm that God's greater glory and the fulfillment of God's holy will was his only object. And he used to say that the divine will was the sovereign law of his heart, and that in this life we must turn our work and action into prayer; that the best possible prayer was to fall in with our Lord's will and accept it wholeheartedly. This really proves that his life was a continual prayer, because I can affirm that he went about his business recollected in God practically all the time. It was easy to tell this although he put on no sad and solemn airs, and only those who knew his ways could tell that he was praying.

About fifteen years ago I once asked him whether he ever went for any length of time without actually and explicitly turning his mind to God, and he said: "Sometimes for as long as about a quarter of an hour."

I was amazed at that in a prelate who was so busy and had to immerse himself in such varied and important business. He taught the people under his direction to keep returning to the thought of God deliberately and even when they were doing things directly concerned with him, for instance preaching, hearing confessions, studying, reading, and talking about spiritual things, and so on.

He told me one day that he stood before kings and princes without feeling any constraint or changing his usual attitude in any way, for he was always in the presence of much greater majesty, and this kept him equally reverent everywhere; and that although, as a rule, he led a busy life surrounded by people, he always kept his heart hidden in God as far as he could. "There are people all round me," he once wrote to me, "and yet my heart is solitary.". . .

He told me he woke to the thought of God and fell asleep in the same way if he could. He also said that he loved to be alone because God was very close to him then, and he felt his presence more than in the rush of work or when he had to talk. . . .

He was always at one with God, doing everything purely for love of him and with no other end in view.

St. Jane de Chantal
A *Testimony*

4

Bloom Where You're Planted

DON'T WASTE YOUR TIME ON USELESS DESIRES

If a young man desires earnestly to be provided with some job before time, to what purpose will this desire serve him? To what purpose does a married woman desire to be a religious? If I desire to buy the property of my neighbor before he is willing to sell it, am I not wasting my time in this desire? Being sick, if I desire to preach or say Mass, visit the sick and do the work of those who are in good health, are not these desires impractical since during this time, it is not possible for me to realize them? Moreover, these worthless desires occupy the place of others which I ought to have: to be very patient, very resigned, very mortified, very obedient and very gentle in my sufferings. This is what God wants me to practice at such a time. Generally we desire like expectant mothers for fresh cherries in autumn and for fresh grapes in winter.

I do not approve in any way that a person bound to some duty or occupation distracts himself by desiring a different kind of life than that which is befitting to his duty, or even practices inconsistent with his present state. Indeed, this dissipates the heart and weakens it in carrying out necessary exercises. If I desire the solitude of the Carthusians, I waste my time. This desire takes the place of the one that I must have to accomplish well in my present charge. Likewise, I would not even wish that we desire better talent and better judgment, because these desires are silly. They take the place of that desire which we should have to improve our own talent such as it is. We are not to desire the means of serving God which we do not have. Instead we are to use faithfully those which we have. . . .

Do not desire crosses except insofar as you have borne those which were offered to you. It is an error to desire martyrdom without having enough courage to bear an insult. The enemy often arouses in us ardent desires for things that are absent and may never come on our way. It is to turn away our minds from present objects from which, however small they may be, we could draw great profit. In imagination we fight monsters in Africa. But in fact, due to lack of attention, we allow ourselves to be killed by little serpents on our way. Do not desire temptations, for it will be rashness. Rather, engage your heart in awaiting them courageously and in defending yourself from them when they come. . . .

When your spirit is purified, feeling itself freed from evil dispositions, it has enormous hunger for spiritual things. In a state of starvation, it desires a thousand kinds of spiritual exercises and practices of mortification, of penance, of humility, of charity, of prayer. It is a good sign, dear Philothea, thus to have a keen appetite, but see whether you can digest well all that you wish to eat. Choose then, from among so many desires . . . what can be practiced and accomplished now. Turn these into good account. Once you do this, God will send you other desires which you will realize in their own time. Thus you will not waste your time in useless desires. . . . Put into effect those which are ripe and in season. ∾

St. Francis de Sales,
Introduction to the Devout Life

LET US DO GOD'S WILL—JOYFULLY!

Besides the general commandments, everyone must carefully observe the particular commandments of their state in life. Whoever doesn't do this—even if he should raise the dead—lives in a state of sin. . . . For example, bishops are commanded to visit their sheep—to teach, correct, console. I may pass the whole week in prayer; I may fast all my life. But if I don't do what I'm commanded, I am lost. . . .

No vocation is without its irksome, bitter, and disagreeable aspects. And furthermore, except for those who are fully resigned to the will of God, everyone would willingly exchange their condition for someone else's. Bishops would prefer not to be bishops; married people would like to be unmarried; single people would like to be married. Where does this general discontent come from, if not from a certain dislike of constraint and a perversity of spirit that makes us think everyone else is better off than we are?

But it all comes to the same thing: turn and turn though we may, we'll never have rest unless we're fully resigned. People who have a fever aren't comfortable anywhere; they haven't been in one bed a quarter of an hour when they want to move to another. It's not the bed that's at fault, but the fever that everywhere torments them. A person who doesn't suffer from the fever of self-will is satisfied with everything, provided that God is served. He doesn't care in what capacity God uses him, provided that he's doing the divine will. It's all one to him.

But this is not all: we must not only will to do the will of God, but in order to be holy, we must do it joyfully. If I were not a bishop, knowing what I know now, perhaps I wouldn't want to be one. But since I am one, not only am I obligated to do what this trying vocation requires: I must do it joyously. I must take pleasure in it and be contented. St. Paul says this: "Let each one stay in his vocation before God" (1 Corinthians 7:24).

We don't have to carry other people's crosses, but only our own. In order for that to happen, our Lord wants us to renounce ourselves—that is, our own will (cf. Matthew 16:24). "I'd like this or that. I'd be better here or there": those are temptations. Our Lord knows well what he is doing. Let us do what he wills; let us stay where he has placed us. ❧

St. Francis de Sales
Letters to Persons in the World

ON NOT FLEEING PEOPLE WHO ANNOY US

From two separate letters to religious superiors who were each dealing with a nun they found troublesome:

My dearest daughter, now you have just the right opportunity for becoming holy. You do indeed need great courage for it, but God will, I trust, give you more every day. Don't be discouraged, but take advantage of this splendid opportunity provided by God to enable you to grow in true humility, gentleness, patience, and above all, . . . the incomparable virtue of putting up with people you find offensive and tiresome. Turn your thoughts often to our good Savior as he endured the various sufferings of his Passion. See how he was mocked, despised, slandered, and then how he said: "Father, forgive them, for they do not know what they do" (Luke 23:34).

Dearest daughter, this poor creature certainly doesn't know what she's doing either, for her temper carries her away. But have patience. Go to our Lord. Entrust completely into his sacred hands the responsibility that he has given you—and especially the care of this poor soul. Rely on him and you will soon see calm restored and your house full of blessings. . . . To have one black sheep is nothing. . . .

This is a person who needs great encouragement and soothing. I beg you, then, to seek her out a little while after her outbursts have passed—a few hours later, perhaps. Go to her to encourage and help her return to the right path, saying kind words with great gentleness and cordiality. You see, my dear daughter, this is a case that calls for not just ordinary but very extraordinary kindness, and you are called on to show it.

Do this willingly, for it may be that you will render greater service to God by your efforts to gain this soul than by everything else you have done in your life. Give her all the time she needs to unburden her heart to you; she will certainly waste your time, but nothing can be done about that. . . . Never let her see that you find her a burden. Don't look impatient or irritated at what she may say or do. Always treat her with great motherliness . . . . I know quite well that you do all this, but I ask you to do it more and more, because I believe with such help she is destined for eternal salvation.

St. Jane de Chantal
The Spirit of Saint Jane Frances de Chantal

SIMPLY OBEY!

One must obey equally in great and little things, in easy and in difficult ones, and remain firm, that is, attached to the cross where obedience has placed us, without accepting or admitting any condition which tries to make us descend from it, no matter how fine it may appear. . . .

Let married people remain on their cross of obedience, which is in marriage. It is the best and most practical cross for them and one of the most demanding, in that there is almost continual activity—and occasions for suffering are more frequent in this state than in any other. Do not desire, therefore, to descend from this cross under any pretext whatever. Since God has placed you there, remain there always.

Let not the prelate or the priest desire to be detached from his cross because of the turmoil of a thousand cares and hindrances he encounters there. Let him attend to his duties of state, taking care of the souls that God has confided to him, instructing some, consoling others, sometimes speaking, sometimes keeping silent, giving time to action and to prayer. This is the cross to which God has attached him. He must remain there firmly, without believing in anything that might induce him to leave it.

Let the religious remain constantly and faithfully nailed to the cross of his vocation, never permitting the least thought that might divert him or make him change the resolution he has made to serve God in this way of life. . . . And do not say to me: "O God! if only I had my way, I would pray for hours and receive so many comforting feelings that I might even experience being enraptured. If I could only pray at this hour, I could easily wrest the very heart of God and place it in my own, or soar up to the cross and place my hand in the Savior's side. . . . If I could only pray *now*, I would pray so fervently that I would be raised right off the ground." All this is nothing but the *appearance* of virtue. We must reject all that is contrary to obedience, never permitting such movements and inspirations. Simply obey. God does not ask anything else of you.

St. Francis de Sales,
Sermons for Lent

PRACTICAL POINTERS FOR A CONTENTED LIFE

From a letter to a married woman:

1. Every day, either in the morning or an hour or two before supper, meditate on the life and death of our Lord. . . . Your meditation should last no more than a good half-hour. At the end of it, always think about the obedience that our Lord showed toward God his Father. You'll find that everything he did was done to fulfill his Father's will. By reflecting on this, make an effort to obtain a great love for the will of God.

2. Before beginning to carry out those duties of your state in life that are trials to you, recall that the saints joyfully did things far greater and harder. Some suffered martyrdom, others the dishonor of the world. St. Francis and many religious of our age kissed and kissed again a thousand times people afflicted with leprosy and sores; others lived in deserts; others with the soldiers on galley ships. All of this they did to please God. And what do we do that even comes close to such difficulties?

3. Think often that all we do has its true value from our conformity with the will of God. If I'm eating and drinking because it's God's will for me to do it, I'm more pleasing to God than if I were to die without having that intention.

4. Often during the day, ask God to give you love of your vocation, and say like St. Paul when he was converted, "Lord, what will you have me do?" (cf. Acts 9:6). "Will you have me serve you in the lowest ministry of your house? Oh, I'll be only too happy to do so; I don't care what I do, provided that I'm serving you." And coming to the particular thing that troubles you, say, "Do you want me to do this? Lord, although I'm not worthy, I'll do it most willingly." And thus you practice great humility. What a treasure you'll gain! Undoubtedly greater than you can imagine.

5. Consider how many saints have been married people like you, and how they accepted this vocation with great sweetness and surrender. . . . Sarah, Rebecca, St. Anne, St. Elizabeth, St. Monica, St. Paula, and a hundred thousand others. Let this encourage you, and ask for their prayers.

We must love what God loves. He loves our vocation, so let us also love it and not waste time thinking about other people's. Let us do our duty. Each person's cross is not too much for him or her. Be both Martha and Mary. Diligently carry out your duties, and often recollect yourself and put yourself in spirit at the feet of our Lord. Say, "My Lord, whether I'm rushing around or staying still, I am all yours and you are all mine. You are my first Spouse, and whatever I do is for love of you."

St. Francis de Sales
Letters to Persons in the World

5

Easy Does It!

Don't Be Too Eager
for Perfection

It is certainly a great pity to see people—and there are only too many of them—who, while aiming at perfection, imagine that it consists in a great multitude of desires. They are always eagerly searching for a way to become perfect, now here, now there. They are never contented or tranquil, for as soon as they have formed one desire they try to conceive another. They are like hens, which have no sooner laid one egg than they start busying themselves to lay another, without attempting to sit on the first. . . . If the hen hatches out a brood, she is quite excited and clucks loudly and incessantly. . . . So, too, there are people who never cease clucking and bustling over their little ones—that is, over their desires of perfection. They can never find enough people to talk to about them and to ask for suitable and novel measures for reaching it. They waste so much time discussing the perfection they're aiming at that they forget to practice the principal means of achieving it: to remain calm and cast all their confidence on God, who alone can give the increase to what is sown and planted (cf. 1 Corinthians 3:6–7).

All our well-being depends on the grace of God, in which we should place all our confidence. And yet, from the overeagerness that these people display to do a great deal, it would seem that they trust in their own labors and in the quantity of devotional practices which they undertake. . . .

Let us not be at all overeager in our work, for in order to do it well we must apply ourselves to it carefully indeed, but calmly and peacefully. We must not put our trust in our efforts, but in God and his grace. Those anxious searchings of heart about becoming perfect and those attempts to determine whether we're making progress are not at all pleasing to God. They only serve to satisfy our self-love, that subtle tormentor which grasps at so much but accomplishes almost nothing. One single good work done with a tranquil spirit is worth far more than several done with overeagerness.

St. Francis de Sales
Spiritual Conferences

WANT WHAT GOD WANTS, WHEN GOD WANTS

From a letter to a nobleman:

Good wants you to temper your overeagerness by calming all this ardor, reducing it to a simple assent of your will to do good quietly—and only because it is God's will. In the same way, yield lovingly to this divine will when it allows you to fail to perform some good deed or to commit some fault. Resign yourself to not being able to resign yourself as completely and utterly as you would like, or as you think our Lord would like.

I don't know if I'm making myself clear. What I mean is that in all your good works you should unite yourself to the will of God's good pleasure, and in your faults and imperfections, you should unite yourself to his permissive will gently, quietly, and with peace of mind. Our blessed father [Francis de Sales] used to say: "Let us do all the good we can, faithfully, peacefully, and quietly; and when we are unfaithful, let us make up for this failure by humility, but a humility that is gentle and tranquil." You know this better than I, dearest brother, and I know this is what you do. But one can always do better. Abandon all your desires for advancement and perfection; hand them over completely into God's hands. Leave the care of them to *him*, and only yearn for as much perfection as he wishes to give you. I beg you, toss away all such desires because they will only cause you worry and disquiet, and even make it possible for self-love to creep in imperceptibly. Have only a pure, simple, peaceful longing to please God, and, as I have said before, this will lead you to act without such impetuosity and overeagerness, but with peace and gentleness. Your chief care ought to be to acquire this spirit; however, this care must be tender and loving, free of anxiety, even as you wait for results with unlimited patience and total dependence on the grace of God. Trust him to bring about these results at the right time for his glory and your benefit. Do not wish to possess them any sooner. In his goodness, he will be a thousand times more pleased to have you rest in his care, surrendered to his holy will, than to have you suffer all sorts of torments in an effort to acquire that perfection you desire so much. ∽

St. Jane de Chantal
Letters of Spiritual Direction

ANTIDOTE FOR ANXIETY

Anxiety is the greatest evil that can befall us except sin. Sedition and internal troubles ruin a nation utterly and prevent it from being able to resist a foreign invasion. Similarly, when we are troubled and restless we lose our power to maintain the virtue which we have acquired. We also lose the means of resisting the temptations of the enemy who then makes every effort to fish, as they say, in troubled waters.

Anxiety arises from an inordinate desire to be freed from the evil we experience or to acquire the good we hoped for. Yet there is nothing which so aggravates the evil or impedes the good as anxiety and eagerness. Birds remain captive in the nets and traps because, when they are entangled in them, they flutter and struggle wildly in order to escape; by doing that they always entangle themselves the more. Therefore when you are taken up by the desire to be delivered from some evil or to obtain some good, place yourself above all in peace and tranquility. Compose your judgment and your will. Then quietly and gently pursue the object of your desire, taking in order the means which are fitting. And when I say "quite gently," I do not mean negligently but without eagerness, confusion and anxiety. Otherwise, instead of obtaining what you desire, you will spoil everything and get yourself entangled. ∾

St. Francis de Sales
Introduction to the Devout Life

A WATCHFUL EYE, A GENTLE TOUCH

"My soul is in danger if I do not hold it in my hands," our blessed father [Francis de Sales] often said to me (Psalm 119:109). Look often to see whether you have your soul in your hands or whether some emotion, trouble, or unrest has carried it off, he used to tell me. See if you have it in command or if, on the other hand, it has been attracted away. If you see that it has escaped from you, go after it and pick it up again. But remember that you must capture it gently and softly; if you take it by strength of arm, you will frighten it.

This is what the saint taught me, and this is my advice to you. Carry, hold, and carefully keep your soul in your hands, that you may always watch it and keep an eye on its movements. Check often in case some tendency wound it, some hatred spoil it, some unruly passion disturb its steadiness, in case some impure or harmful desire already have robbed you of it. Then, very gently repair the disorder, returning your soul once again to its place, which is God, its true center.

Also check to see if your soul is well disposed to everything that might please God and is quite submissive to all he permits. Is it content and equally accepting of sweet or bitter, of whatever is God's good will and pleasure? Look again to see if this dear soul is in a state to be given back to the Lord who gave it, whenever he demands it of you. In short, I urge you to imitate those who carry in their hands things they are afraid to lose: they hold them carefully, examine them often, and expose them to no danger of being lost. Similarly, examine your soul often and don't expose it to dangers. Thus, you will carry and hold it in hand. And this is our great happiness—to have and hold something so precious as our souls. ❧

> St. Jane de Chantal
> *Her Exhortations,*
> *Conferences and Instructions*

A GENTLE AND HUMBLE HEART

From a letter to a married woman of the upper class:

Yes, truly, ever so gently we must continue to cut out of our lives all that is superfluous and worldly. Don't you see that no one prunes vines by hacking them with an axe but by cutting them very carefully with a pruning hook, one shoot at a time?

I saw a piece of sculpture once that an artist had worked at for ten years before it was completed; during all that time with chisel and burin he never stopped chipping away at everything that was in the way of exact proportions. No, there is no doubt about it, we cannot possibly arrive in a day where we aspire to be. We have to take this step today; tomorrow, another; and thus, step by step, achieve self-mastery, which is no small victory.

I beg you, keep up confidently and sincerely this holy pursuit. . . . How happy you will be if in the midst of the world you keep Jesus Christ in your heart! I beg him to live and rule there eternally.

Keep in mind the main lesson he left us—in *three* words so that we would never forget it and could repeat it a hundred times a day: "Learn of me," he said, "that I am gentle and humble of heart." (Matthew 11:29). That says it all: to have a heart gentle toward one's neighbor and humble toward God. At every moment give this heart, the very heart of your heart, to our Savior. You will see that as this divine, delicate Lover takes his place in your heart, the world with its vanities and superfluities will leave.

I have said this to you in person, madam, and now I write it: I don't want a devotion that is bizarre, confused, neurotic, strained, and sad, but rather, a gentle, attractive, peaceful piety; in a word, a piety that is quite spontaneous and wins the love of God, first of all, and after that, the love of others. ∾

St. Francis de Sales
Letters of Spiritual Direction

STRATEGY FOR CALMING EMOTIONAL STORMS

What should we do when we feel all our emotions suddenly rising up in turmoil? We must not force ourselves to undertake many measures in order to conquer them and bring them back to duty; if we do that, they may get the better of us. Rather, in the highest part of our soul, we must simply join ourselves to God's will, humble ourselves and, from that moment, keep close to

God in peace and in the greatest tranquility we can manage. We must do as our threshers did today on board their boat, which was carrying our wheat on the lake. Suddenly they found themselves in great peril: a violent storm arose in an instant and threatened to sink them with the boat and everything on it. What did they do? They did not obstinately set themselves to go straight against the current through these great waves. If they had done that, they would have been lost. Instead, they followed the little waves and very skillfully, very gently, brought their boat to shore. They managed to land by avoiding the storm, not by battling against it.

Here is a little model of what we should do when we are taken by surprise as we row peacefully in our little boat. When all our emotions arise to stir up a great internal storm that seems certain to overwhelm us or drag us after it, we must not wish to calm this tempest ourselves. Rather, we must gently draw near the shore, keeping our will firmly in God, and coast along the little waves; by humble knowledge of ourselves, we will reach God, who is our sure port. Let us go gently along without agitation and anxiety and without giving in to our emotions. By doing so, we shall make it to that divine port—with some delay, but with more glory than if we had enjoyed perfect calm and had navigated our little boat without any challenges.

St. Jane de Chantal
Her Exhortations,
Conferences and Instructions

ON SEEING THINGS IN PERSPECTIVE

We will soon be in eternity, and then we will see how inconsequential all the things of this world are and how little it matters whether they turn out or not. At present, however, we apply ourselves to them as if they were great things. When we were little children, with what eagerness we assembled little bits of tile, wood, and mud to make houses and small buildings! And if someone destroyed them, we were very sad and cried over it; now, though, we know well that it all mattered very little. One day it will be the same with us in heaven: we will see that our concerns in this world were really just child's play.

I don't want to detract from the care that we should take regarding these little trifles, because God has entrusted them to us in this world as an exercise. But I would indeed like to take away the passion and anxiety of this care. Since we're children, let's carry on with our child's play, but let's not trouble ourselves to death over these games. And if someone destroys our little houses and little plans, let's not torment ourselves greatly over it. When that night comes in which we will all have to take shelter—I'm talking about death—all these little houses will be of no use to us; we will have to take shelter in the house of our Father. Attend faithfully to your duties, but know that your most important business is to tend to your salvation and make progress on the saving path of true devotion.

Be patient with everyone, but especially with yourself. What I mean to say is don't trouble yourself about your imperfections, and always have the courage to lift yourself out of them. I'm pleased that you begin again every day: there is no better way to live out the spiritual life than always to begin again and never to think you have done enough. ❧

> St. Francis de Sales
> *Letters to Persons in the World*

GENTLE VIOLENCE WINS THE KINGDOM

It is impossible to enter into heaven and to be saved unless you do violence to yourself. Our Lord himself has said: "It is only the violent who bear it away" (Matthew 11:12). I repeat this so that, knowing this truth, you may engrave in your heart the internal resolve to spare yourself in nothing. You must conquer and use force with yourself in order to become virtuous . . . at the cost of all your natural tendencies. Still, this violence must be gentle though strong. . . .

And yet there is no escaping it: we must do violence to ourselves. If God has hidden the prize of eternal glory, which is an infinite good, in our victory over self, how can we fail to attempt self-mastery? How dare we think of playing the coward?

You know that it takes work and attention to learn any art—even a common one. Look at the young boy who wants to be a shoemaker. How many times a day must he put aside his own preferences? All day he must sit hunched over, tediously working his arms; he must endure being beaten. Look at the person who wants to be a doctor; he might put in as many as twenty years before coming to the end of his studies. None of this, however, can compare with our calling, nor are there any studies aimed at a holier, higher, and purer goal than ours. For our goal is the union of our soul with God, the perfection of our vocation, and the attainment of solid virtues, riches that endure forever and even accompany us to heaven.

We must therefore labor, but with faithful, constant, earnest, sweet, and loving toil. We are working for God, and it is to gain eternity that we fight against ourselves. ⚬

> St. Jane de Chantal
> *Her Exhortations,*
> *Conferences and Instructions*

6

Total Trust

ABANDON YOURSELF ENTIRELY TO GOD

Our Lord loves with a most tender love those who are fortunate enough to abandon themselves completely to his fatherly care, letting themselves be governed by his divine providence—without any idle speculations as to whether it will be useful to them and to their advantage or painful to them and to their loss. This is because they are well assured that nothing can be sent, nothing permitted by this paternal and most loving heart which will not be good and beneficial to them. All that is required is that they place all their confidence in him and say from their heart, "Into your blessed hands I commend my spirit, my soul, my body and all that I have. Do with them as you please." . . .

Once you have given yourself entirely into the hands of God, you have only to remain close to our Lord without troubling yourself about anything that concerns either your body or your soul. For since you have committed yourself to God's providence, why do you need to think about what will become of you? Our Lord, to whom you have surrendered yourself completely, will think of everything for you. (I don't, however, mean to say that we must not think about the things to which we are bound by our respective duties; it wouldn't be right . . . to neglect whatever is necessary for carrying out the duties of our state in life.)

It is quite true that it takes a very great confidence to abandon ourselves unreservedly to divine providence in this way; but then, when we abandon everything, our Lord takes care of everything and arranges everything. On the other hand, if we reserve anything to ourselves instead of confiding it to him, he leaves it to us, saying, as it were: "You think yourselves wise enough to manage this matter without me. Well, I will leave you to do so. You will see how you will succeed." . . .

The soul that has surrendered itself . . . has only to rest in the arms of our Lord like a child on his mother's breast. When she puts him down to walk, he walks until she picks him up again; when she wishes to carry him, he allows her to do so. He neither knows nor thinks about where he is going, but allows himself to be carried or led wherever his mother pleases. ∾

St. Francis de Sales
Spiritual Conferences

In Physical Suffering, Trust Him

God's most holy will is best of all: he knows how to draw his glory and your eternal salvation out of this suffering. Surrender yourself completely to the care and the everlasting love God has for you. This is your part: you should do this and nothing but this. Leave soul, body, and mind absolutely in his hands. Have no fear of losing your mind through the violence of your pain, for God knows your capacity. He will not allow more than you can bear. If it pleases him to permit this affliction, you should submit lovingly to it. Give yourself up entirely and without reserve to his most holy purposes so that he may deal with you and everything about you according to his will. In this is all our happiness.

Act in this way, for I assure you that if you knew the value of your infirmity you would cherish it more than all the good things of earth.

St. Jane de Chantal
The Spirit of Saint Jane Frances de Chantal

Use the Grace Given to You

Most certainly, God gives everyone sufficient grace for doing all that he wants us to do. People respond to it in different ways, however, and not everyone uses the grace that is given to them. . . .

Tell me, if you were mothers of families, would you send your servants and your children to work in the fields or prune the vines without providing them with the tools necessary for doing what you wanted them to do? My son, Celse-Bénigne—if I had not supplied him with whatever he required when I told him to do something—would have said to me, "Mother, give me this or that, and I will do as you say." Are we to think that God asks us to do something and does not at the same time give us the assistance necessary for carrying out his commands? It would be a great mistake to have such mistrust. No, God is never wanting to us. ∾

> St. Jane de Chantal
> *Her Exhortations,*
> *Conferences and Instructions*

ASK FOR NOTHING, REFUSE NOTHING

Go, full of courage, to do whatever you are called to do, but go in simplicity. If you have any fears, say to yourself, "The Lord will provide for me" (Genesis 22:8). If your weakness troubles you, cast yourself on God and trust in him. The apostles were for the most part ignorant fishermen, but God educated them for the responsibility he wanted to give them. Trust in him, lean on his providence, and fear nothing. Do not say, "I have no talent for speaking." No matter, go without protest, for God will give you what to say and do when the time comes. Even if you have no virtues or perceive none in yourself, don't be distressed on that account, for if you undertake . . . any work, whatever it may be, for the glory of God and out of obedience, he will take care of you and has pledged himself to provide everything you will need. . . .

I have a very strong desire to engrave on your mind a saying that is incomparably useful: Ask for nothing and refuse nothing. Receive what is given to you and do not ask for what is not offered to you. . . . In this practice you will find peace for your soul (cf. Matthew 11:29). Keep your heart in this state of holy indifference, ready to receive all that will be given you and desiring nothing that will not. In a word, desire nothing. Rather, leave yourself and all your affairs completely and absolutely in the care of divine providence.

Allow yourself to be dealt with by that providence exactly as children let their nurses deal with them. Let it carry you, as it were, on the right arm or on the left as it pleases, for this is what a child does. Leave it free to lay you down or pick you up, for it is a good mother and knows what you need better than you do yourself. I mean that if divine providence allows you to experience trials or opportunities to die to yourself, you must not refuse; accept them courageously, lovingly, and calmly. If [none] . . . come to you, then don't desire or ask for them. In the same way, if you are given comforting experiences of God's presence, receive them in a spirit of gratitude, recognizing that they come from God's goodness. If you have none, don't desire them.

Try to keep your heart prepared to accept every event as sent by divine providence. As far as possible, view them all with an equal mind. . . . I am, of course, speaking of earthly things; as regards virtues, we may and should desire them and ask God for them: the love of God encompasses them all. ❧

St. Francis de Sales
Spiritual Conferences

GOD PROVIDES FOR ALL HIS CHILDREN

From a letter to her married daughter:

You are too attached to the things of this life and take them too much to heart. What do you have to be afraid of? Is it that the fact of having so many children deprives you of the means of providing for and educating them according to their birth and your ambition? Have no such fears, I beg of you, for in this you wrong God who gives them to you and who is good enough and rich enough to nourish them and provide for them in a way that advances his glory and their salvation. That is all we should desire for our children. . . .

Now, my dearest daughter, look lovingly on all these little creatures as entrusted to you by God. . . . Care for them, cherish them tenderly, and bring them up not in vanity but faithfully, in the fear of

God. By doing this and entrusting all these anxieties of yours to divine providence, you will see how sweetly and tenderly all will be provided for. You will see that you have good reason to bless and rely wholly on God's providence. Take my advice, dearest daughter, and throw yourself into these safe arms. Serve God, cast vanity aside, live in perfect harmony with the husband God has given you, interest yourself in overseeing your household well, apply yourself to that work actively and diligently, and begin from this day on to live according to the ways and practices of a true mother. If I had not had the courage to do this from the beginning in my married life, we should not have had enough to live on, for we had a smaller income than you, and we were fifteen thousand crowns in debt.

Be brave then, dearest daughter. Use your time and your mind not in worrying and being anxious about the future but in serving God and your household, for such is his will. Do this, and you will see all that you do marked by blessings.

St. Jane de Chantal
Selected Letters

We Must Not Be Afraid of Fear

To a man recovering from illness but suffering from deep depression:

I imagine your mind is still preoccupied with some fear of sudden death and of the judgments of God. What a dreadful torment this is! My soul, which endured it for six weeks, is very capable of sympathizing with those who suffer from it.

But, sir, I must speak a little with you, heart to heart, and tell you that whoever has a true desire to serve our Lord and avoid sin should not get anxious at all with the thought of death or of the divine judgments. Although both are to be feared, still the fear should not be of that terrible and terrifying nature which beats down and depresses the vigor and strength of the soul. It should be a fear so mixed with confidence in the goodness of God that it becomes gentle.

And, sir, we shouldn't doubt whether we can trust in God when we find it difficult to keep from sin, or when we imagine or fear that we might not be able to resist in certain situations and temptations. Oh no, sir, for distrust of our strength is not a failure of resolution, but a true acknowledgment of our misery.

I say that if we felt we should have neither strength nor courage to resist temptation if it presented itself to us now, provided that we desired to resist it and hoped that if it came God would help us, and if we asked his help, we must by no means be upset. It is not always necessary to feel strength and courage. It is enough to hope and desire to have them at the right time and place. It is not necessary to feel in ourselves any sign or any mark that we shall have this courage. It is enough that we hope God will help us. . . .

God, who does nothing in vain, does not give us the strength or the courage when there is no need to use them. At the necessary time, though, nothing is wanting. Therefore, we must always hope that in all situations God will help us if we call on him. And we should always use the words of David, "Why are you sorrowful, my soul, and why do you trouble me? Hope in the Lord" (Psalm 42:5) and his prayer, "When my strength fails, O Lord, forsake me not" (Psalm 71:9).

Well, then, since you desire to be entirely God's, why are you fearful of your weakness, in which you are to put no sort of trust? Don't you hope in God? Will the person who trusts in him ever be put to shame (cf. Psalm 31:1)? No, sir, never. I beg you to quell all the objections you might have. You do not need to give them any other answer than that you desire to be faithful on all occasions and that you hope God will make you so. There is no need to test your spirit to see whether it would be faithful or not. These tests are illusory. Many people who are valiant when they don't see the enemy are not valiant in his presence; on the other hand, many who are afraid before battle are filled with courage by the actual danger. We must not fear fear. ✺

> St. Francis de Sales
> *Letters to Persons in the World*

SUSTAINED BY THE HOPE OF HEAVEN

In my talks with the blessed father [Francis de Sales], I saw plainly that God had given him a happy, tender and constant love for the good things promised to us in the life to come. He looked forward to them with humble trust in God's mercy and in the merits of our Lord's holy Passion. His spirit was constantly bent on the bliss of eternity. I think this comes out in hundreds of his letters. He openly confessed that all he deserved in his own wretchedness was hell, but by the infinite merits of his Lord and Savior's Passion and his great mercy, he humbly and trustfully hoped for the everlasting riches laid up for God's children in heaven. "Won't we all be together in heaven one day?" he used to say to us. "This is my hope and my joy." And one day he wrote to me: "My soul seems to be clinging more and more closely to God now, at least I feel that eternal things and holy charity mean more and more to me."

When things went wrong, as they will do in this life, he used to say: "Be brave and cheer up—we shall soon be in heaven; put your trust firmly in eternal life. What else would you expect our Lord to do with his eternity if he didn't give it to poor, weak little people like us?" He said one day . . . that we must die between two pillows: our humble confession that all we deserve is hell, and our perfect trust in God's mercy which will give us paradise.

I remember one day when I was dangerously ill the blessed father came to comfort and assist me in my last journey, and he told me to rest my head at the foot of the cross like a small lizard, getting the benefit of the precious blood flowing down on me, and trusting utterly in our Lord's mercy. . . .

Another time he said: "You see, when dear friends die, this is surely a happy thing because it helps to fill heaven and increase our King's glory. Some day, which only God knows, we shall go and join them; and while we're waiting, let us work hard to learn the song of love and then we can sing it more perfectly in an eternity of bliss."

"O God," he said on another occasion, "how happy I am to feel so sure that we shall one day be eternally united in our will to love and praise God! May God's providence lead us where it will, but I hope, no, I'm sure that we shall reach our haven and get there in the end, yes, quite sure, thanks be to God. May we serve him with gladness, and be glad but not careless, sure of ourselves but not brash."

One stormy day when he was crossing the Lake of Geneva in a small, light craft, he said how very happy he was to think that providence apart, he had nothing between him and death except a few frail planks of timber. "Divine providence is my soul's only trysting place. O God, you have taught me this lesson from my youth upward, and even now I will declare your wonderful works" (Psalm 71:17). ∽

St. Jane de Chantal
A Testimony

THE HIDDEN REALITY

We are always in God's presence but not always attentive to it, which is the reason we sin against him. Our blessed father [Francis de Sales] used to say, "If a blind man is in an apartment where the king is, he goes on joking as usual, unless they tell him that the king is there; then, although he doesn't see him, . . . he becomes attentive, respectful and reverent." We are in this world as poor blind men. . . . We don't see our Lord, but faith teaches us that God is present in all things . . . and, moreover, that he dwells in our hearts in a particular way. . . . But, alas, we are blind! Dear God, since we don't see you, we easily forget your divine presence. For this there is no remedy except to stir up our faith often that God is present everywhere and that nothing happens in the world unless it is ordained by his divine providence, which governs the whole world according to his good pleasure.

Persons who are aware of this truth will never be disturbed. "Well," they may say, "I know that God is present with me, that he is more in me than myself. I know that he governs all things and that his eye watches over all. I know that nothing happens in heaven or earth unless he ordains or permits it. Therefore, if the waters of the lake swell and submerge the monastery, I know that God is present with me and that he permits this flood for some reason which it belongs to him to know. Why, then, should I be troubled? O God, you rule the waves, the sky, and the earth. If you allow me to be drowned or burned, I consent with my whole heart. . . . In silence of spirit, I adore and revere all your hidden judgments."

> St. Jane de Chantal
> *Her Exhortations,*
> *Conferences and Instructions*

7

When God Seems Far Away

FAITH AND FEELINGS: A CRUCIAL DISTINCTION

If I am not mistaken, when we say that we can't find God and that he seems so far away, we only mean that we can't feel his presence. . . . Many people do not distinguish between God and the feeling of God, between faith and the feeling of faith—which is a very great problem. It seems to them that when they do not feel God they are not in his presence. This is a mistake. A person . . . about to suffer martyrdom for God . . . does not actually think of him but rather of his pain . . . . Although the feeling of faith may be wanting, he makes an act of great love. There is a difference between . . . being in God's presence and having the feeling of his presence. God alone can give the latter. As to my being able to give you the means of obtaining this feeling, it is impossible.

St. Francis de Sales
Spiritual Conferences

LOOKED UPON WITH LOVE

From a letter to a nun:

You are wondering, my very dear daughter, if our Lord can be thinking of you and looking at you lovingly? Yes, my very dear daughter, he is thinking about you and not only about you but about every hair of your head: this is an article of faith and you must not have the slightest doubt about it. I know of course that you do not really doubt it but that this is just your way of expressing the aridity, dryness and indifference that you now feel. . . . Indeed, God "is in this place and I knew it not," said Jacob (Genesis 28:16); that is to say, I did not see it and I could not in any way feel it, it did not seem possible to me. . . .

And you have no cause to doubt that he is looking upon you with love; for he looks lovingly upon the most horrible sinners in the world, even if they have very little real desire for conversion. And tell me, my very dear daughter, isn't it your intention to belong to God? Don't you want to serve him faithfully? . . .

You are right in saying that this is a temptation, my very dear daughter, in that your heart has no tender feeling towards God; for tenderness would mean consolation and consolation would mean the end of your unhappiness. But love of God, my daughter, does not consist either in consolation or in tender feelings; else our Lord would not have loved his Father when he was sad unto death and cried out: "My Father, my Father, why have you forsaken me?" (Matthew 27:46). And it was then that he was making the greatest act of love we can possibly conceive. . . .

Come now, my very dear daughter, this is enough for today. Live joyfully: our Lord's eyes are on you and he is looking at you lovingly, all the more tenderly because you are so helpless. Never allow your will to nurture contrary thoughts; and when they bother you, do not look at them in themselves, turn your eyes away from their wickedness and turn towards God with brave humility, speaking to him about his indescribable goodness which makes him love our poor, feeble, and lowly human nature in spite of its weaknesses. ❧

St. Francis de Sales
Selected Letters

TURNING FROM DISTRACTIONS

There is no need to get upset and blame ourselves because we have difficulty in our prayer, or to think that it is useless and displeasing to God. No, not if we have been faithful to it. Here is an example that will make this plain: it is that of good Abraham, the great patriarch, for whom I have much love and fondness.

Abraham often used to offer sacrifices and burnt offerings to the Lord. One day as he was offering a sacrifice, birds of prey landed on the carcasses (cf. Genesis 15:11).

Seeing this, Abraham took a stick and untiringly drove them away as best he could. This went on for the duration of the sacrifice. Suppose Abraham had complained to God afterwards and said, "Lord, what a poor sacrifice I've offered you in the midst of the distractions caused by the birds of prey!" Certainly, the Lord would have answered that he had not stopped being pleased with the patriarch's offering. The situation had come about against Abraham's will, and he had done everything in his power to drive the birds away. . . .

So when we pray and have a multitude of distractions like troublesome flies, as long as they displease us and we do what lies in our power to turn from them faithfully, our prayer doesn't stop being good and acceptable to God. We may be sure of this. When we have a sense of our sinfulness at prayer, there is no need to make speeches to our Lord to inform him. It is better to remain quietly in this state, which speaks to God for us sufficiently. . . . Draw near to God with the greatest simplicity you can, and be certain that the simplest prayer is the best.

> St. Jane de Chantal
> *Her Exhortations,*
> *Conferences and Instructions*

When Prayer Is Dry

It may happen, Philothea, that you find no liking for meditation nor any consolation in it. I plead with you, do not be upset in the least. Sometimes open the door to vocal prayers: tell the Lord about your unhappy condition, acknowledge your unworthiness, ask him for his help, kiss his picture if you have it, speak to him these words of Jacob: I will not let you go, Lord, unless you bless me (Genesis 32:26). . . .

On other occasions, get hold of a book and read it attentively until your spirit awakens and is better disposed. Sometimes arouse your heart by some attitude and gesture of exterior devotion: prostrate yourself on the ground, cross your hands upon your breast, kiss a crucifix. . . .

Even if after all this you receive no comfort, do not be worried, no matter how great your dryness. Continue to remain before God in a devout attitude. So many courtiers go a hundred times a year into the audience hall of the prince, without hope of speaking to him but only to be seen by him and to fulfill their duty. We should come to holy prayer in the same way, my dear Philothea, purely and simply to fulfill our duty and as an expression of our faithfulness.

If the divine Majesty is pleased to speak to us and carry on a conversation with us by his holy inspirations and interior consolations, it will surely be for us a great honor and a most delightful pleasure. But if it does not please him to do us such a favor, leaving us there without speaking to us, as if he had not seen us and as if we were not in his presence, we must not go away for this reason. On the contrary, we must remain there, before this supreme Goodness, with a disposition that is devout and calm.

Then, he will most certainly be pleased with our patience and observe our devoted attention and perseverance. So, another time, when we come before him again, he will show favor to us and converse with us by his consolations, making us experience the delight of holy prayer. But when he does not do so, let us be happy, Philothea, that it is a very great honor indeed to be near him and to be seen by him. ⌇

St. Francis de Sales
Introduction to the Devout Life

A SILENT FLAME IN GOD'S PRESENCE

Y ou tell me that you have no thoughts, that you have no feelings toward God. But if it is God himself you hold, why be concerned about anything else? What does there remain for you to desire?

Here you are at prayer. God is granting you nothing whatever. Well, if you did not know how to do anything else, you could adore him, adore his presence, adore his ways, his works; and, for such a prayer, what need is there of great and high thoughts? You adore him better by your silence than by your speeches. If you are incapable of anything whatever, then suffer. If you cannot pray by effort, then you will pray by endurance. In such an extremity, turn your face towards the Blessed Virgin, or towards any of the saints. Beg them to make your prayer for you, or to grant you some share in that prayer which they utter forever in heaven.

Are we then to be entirely idle and inactive in prayer? No, we must submit our minds to the Holy Spirit who means to be our light and our guide. Were you to do no other thing than to stand in the presence of God and consume your life away before him, like a candle burning itself up in the presence of the Sacrament, would you not be blessed and fortunate? ∽

St. Jane de Chantal
St. Chantal on Prayer

PUT EVERYTHING TO GOOD USE

There are people who want to have experiences of God's closeness in prayer as a means of growing holy, . . . but nevertheless he permits them to be dry and parched, powerless and blind to the extent that they don't even know what they're doing. Well, then, let's look for our perfection in this darkness and obscurity, by humility, patience, and resignation. . . . Another person would like to have peace of mind: it seems to her that she would go through her spiritual exercises much better. And yet God permits trouble to befall her—restlessness, distractions, temptations, and other difficulties.

What must be done in these cases? Seek for peace in the midst of your trial, calm your mind in the midst of your restlessness by seeing the will of God in these things and by bending to his good pleasure. This will prepare you to receive the peace you desire so strongly. Deal in this way with every other desire that comes to you, practicing faithfully the holy teaching of our father, Francis de Sales, to refuse nothing that God has given to us for our perfection and to desire nothing that is not given to us. In short, we must be good housewives and put everything to use for our growth, even our own faults and imperfections.

On this subject, I remember what the good Carmelite Mother Louise . . . used to say when she first came to the city of Dijon . . . . "I love the women of Dijon so much because they are so very practical and make so much profit out of anything." Let us do the same, becoming *practical* and profiting by everything, for in this consists our happiness and perfection. 〰️

St. Jane de Chantal
Her Exhortations,
Conferences and Instructions

WHY HAVE YOU FORSAKEN ME?

From a letter to Francis de Sales:

I write because I cannot stop myself from doing so, for this morning I am more tired of myself than usual. My state of my soul is so gravely flawed that, in anguish of spirit, I see myself giving way on every side. Assuredly, my good father, I am almost overwhelmed by the depth of this misery. The presence of God, which was formerly such a delight to me, now makes me tremble all over and shudder with fear. . . . Death itself, it seems to me, would be less painful to bear . . . and I feel as if all things had power to harm me. I am afraid of everything; I live in dread, not because of harm to myself, but because I fear to displease God. Oh, how far away his help seems! Thinking of this I spent last night in great bitterness and could utter no other words than these, "My God, my God, alas! why have you forsaken me?"

At daybreak God gave me a little light. . . . Then trouble rushed back upon me with a mighty force, and all was darkness. . . . Though in utter dryness, I said, "Do, Lord, whatever is pleasing to you. I wish it. Annihilate me, I am content. Overwhelm me, I most sincerely desire it. Tear out, cut, burn, do just as you please, I am yours."

God has shown me that he doesn't take much account of faith that comes of feelings and emotions. This is why, although it goes against my inclinations, I never wish for a feeling of devotion. I don't desire it. God is enough for me. In spite of my absolute misery I hope in him, and I trust that he will continue to support me so that his will may be accomplished in me. ❧

St. Jane de Chantal
Selected Letters

IMITATION OF CHRIST

Think about that great abandonment which our Master suffered in the Garden of Olives. See how this dear Son, having asked his good Father for relief and realizing that he did not want to give it, stops thinking about it, stops striving and seeking after it. As if he had never thought of it, he valiantly and courageously accomplishes the work of our redemption.

After you have prayed to the Father to give you relief, if it does not please him to do it, think of it no more. Brace yourself courageously to work out your salvation on the cross, as if you were never to come down from it and as if you were never again to see the sky of your life clear and serene. . . .

Suppose you were never going to be delivered from your distress. What would you do? You would say to God, "I am yours. If my miseries are agreeable to you, multiply and extend them." I have confidence in God that you would say this and think no more about your troubles; at least you would no longer let yourself get upset. Do this now, and befriend your burden as if you were always going to live with it. You will find that when you are no longer thinking about deliverance, God will think about it. When you are no longer worried, God will be there. ❧

St. Francis de Sales
Letters to Persons in the World

8

So You're Not Perfect

ON PATIENTLY ENDURING OUR IMPERFECTIONS

From a letter to a young woman in a religious community:

I'm sure you can readily see how the interior trials you have experienced were caused by the multiplicity of reflections and desires that came about in your great hurry to attain some imaginary perfection. By this I mean that your imagination had formed an ideal of absolute perfection which your will wanted to reach, but, frightened by the huge difficulty, or rather, impossibility of attaining it, remained, as it were, heavy with child, unable to give birth (cf. 2 Kings 19:3). . . . Slow down, take a few deep breaths, and by reflecting on the dangers you escaped, avert those that might come your way. . . .

Know that patience is the one virtue which gives greatest assurance of our reaching perfection (cf. James 1:4), and, while we must have patience with others, we must also have it with ourselves. Those who aspire to the pure love of God need to be more patient with themselves than with others. We have to endure our own imperfections in order to attain perfection; I say "endure patiently" not "love" or "embrace": humility is nurtured through such endurance.

In truth, we have to admit that we are weak creatures who scarcely do anything well. . . .

Must we, for that reason, be worried, anxious, pressured, distressed? Certainly not. Is it necessary to think up volumes of desires in order to stimulate ourselves to reach this indication of perfection? Of course not. All we need to do is express simple wishes which witness to our gratitude. I can say, "Well, well, so I can't serve and praise God as fervently as the seraphim!" but I mustn't waste time making wishes as if I were going to reach such exquisite perfection in this world, and say, "I want this, I'm going to make every effort to get it, and if I don't, I'm going to be furious!" I don't mean that we shouldn't head in the direction of perfection, but that we mustn't try to get there in a day. . . .

Our imperfections are going to accompany us to the grave. We can't go anywhere without having our feet on the ground, yet we don't just lie there, sprawled [in the dust]. On the other hand, we mustn't think we can fly, for we are like little chicks who don't have wings yet. We die little by little; so our imperfections must die with us, a little each day. Dear imperfections, they force us to acknowledge our misery, give us practice in humility, selflessness, patience, and watchfulness. ∾

St. Francis de Sales
Letters of Spiritual Direction

KNOWLEDGE OF OURSELVES, CONFIDENCE IN GOD

How must we set about reforming our souls? We must really know ourselves—our nothingness, our lowliness, and our sinfulness. If our understanding is filled with this truth, we shall see clearly that we are full of faults, imperfections, and things needing to be changed . . . . In the exercise of Christian virtues, we are like birds that have no wings to fly with and no feet to walk with. We cannot so much as pronounce the name of Jesus without the Lord's special help. . . .

Whenever there is an occasion of doing some good and practicing some virtue, we must acknowledge our powerlessness and inability to act of ourselves. Thus expecting nothing from ourselves but much indeed from God and his grace—which will unfailingly be given to us—we may say boldly with St. Paul, "I can do all things in him who strengthens me" (Philippians 4:13). If we do anything good, we must carefully refer it all back to God, for the glory of it belongs to him. And when we have fallen into a fault and stumbled, we must not be astonished at all. Very gently we must humble ourselves before God, saying, "O Lord, this is what I'm capable of. This is my poverty and misery. This is what I am. . . ."

Truly, it is for lack of self-knowledge that we are astonished to see ourselves fall short. We presume so much; we expect to be able to produce some good in and of ourselves. We are deceived, and sometimes our Lord even permits us to have a very heavy fall so that we may become acquainted with ourselves. . . .

Knowledge of self and confidence in God—this, in my opinion, is how we must begin to reform ourselves. ∞

> St. Jane de Chantal
> *Her Exhortations,*
> *Conferences and Instructions*

I Can Do Nothing, I Can Do Everything

Humility makes us mistrust ourselves; generosity makes us trust in God. Humility and generosity are so closely united that they never are and never can be separated. . . . Without a doubt, the humility that does not produce generosity is false. For, once humility has said, "I can do nothing, I am only absolute nothingness," it suddenly gives place to generosity of spirit which says, "There is nothing and there can be nothing that I am unable to do, so long as I put all my confidence in God, who can do all things." Buoyed up by this confidence, it courageously undertakes to do all that is required. . . .

I can assure you that humility would not consider it impossible to work miracles, if it were commanded to do so. For if someone who is humble sets out to fulfill such a command in simplicity of heart, God will work a miracle rather than fail to provide whatever power is needed to complete the attempt. This is because it is undertaken not through self-reliance but through dependence on the gifts that God has given. And so the humble person reasons in this way: "If God calls me to a state of perfection, ... what can prevent my attaining it, since I am well assured that he who has begun the work of my perfection will finish it?" (cf. Philippians 1:6). But take note that all this is done without any presumption. The confidence I am describing does not make us less on our guard for fear of failing; on the contrary, it makes us all the more watchful over ourselves, more vigilant and careful to do whatever may serve for our growth in holiness.

Humility does not only consist in mistrust of ourselves, but also in confidence in God. Indeed, mistrust of ourselves and of our own strength produces confidence in God, and of this confidence is born that generosity of spirit of which we are speaking. The Blessed Virgin, Our Lady, gives us a striking example of this in the words, "Behold the handmaid of the Lord; let it be done to me according to your word" (Luke 1:38). In calling herself the handmaid of the Lord, she made the greatest possible act of humility, since, in contrast to the angel's praises, . . . she brought forward her own lowliness. . . . Yet observe that as soon as she has paid this debt to humility, she instantly makes an act of perfect generosity. . . . "It's true that I'm not in any respect capable of this grace in and of myself," she would say in explanation. "But since what is good in me is of God and since what you tell me is his most holy will, I believe that it can and will be done." ❧

St. Francis de Sales
Spiritual Conferences

TRUE AND FALSE HUMILITY

Many say that they leave mental prayer to the perfect and they themselves are not worthy to practice it. Some declare that they do not dare to receive Communion often because they do not feel themselves pure enough. Others say that they are afraid of bringing disgrace on devotion by practicing it, because of their great misery and weakness. Others refuse to employ their talents in the service of God and neighbor, because they feel that they know their weakness. In fact, they are afraid of becoming proud if they are instruments of something good, and so while enlightening others, they would burn themselves out. All this is mere pretense and a kind of humility that is not only false but also malicious. By this means, they wish silently and subtly to find fault with the things of God or at all events to conceal self-love, love of their own opinion, their own moods and laziness, under the pretext of humility.

"Ask of God for a sign in heaven above or in the depths of the sea below," says the prophet Isaiah to the unhappy King Ahaz and he answers, No, I will not ask of him at all, I will not tempt the Lord (Isaiah 7:11-12). The wicked man! He pretends to show great reverence for God. Under the color of humility, he excuses himself from aspiring to the grace which divine goodness offers him. But does he not see that it is pride to refuse God's wish to bestow grace upon us? We are obliged to receive the gifts of God and it is humility to obey and follow as closely as possible his desires. Now the desire of God is that we become perfect (cf. Matthew 5:48), uniting ourselves to him and imitating him as closely as we can. The proud man who trusts in himself has good reason for not undertaking anything. The humble man is all the more courageous, the more he realizes that he is powerless; the more he esteems himself worthless, the more daring he becomes, because he puts his whole trust in God who is pleased to exalt his almighty power in our weakness and manifest his mercy in our misery. ❧

St. Francis de Sales
Introduction to the Devout Life

REALITY CHECK

There are people who have their desires and emotions at rest because nothing crosses them. But in fact, solid virtue is acquired only in the midst of contradictions. People cannot say they are patient when they suffer nothing. . . . They are like rivers that flow so gently when the weather is calm and nothing obstructs their course but whose waves arise and make great noise at the least puff of wind. Their calm did not come from themselves but from the fact that the wind did not blow on them. I advise these people to humble themselves a great deal, for their virtue, I assure them, is only a phantom or sham of the real thing.

Our Lord allows them to have strong desires and to fall to the ground in order to keep them humble and little in their own eyes. He makes them know their weakness and what they are without his help. To keep us then in this knowledge, which is so useful to our souls, he permits us to experience the greatest failures when we have formed the best resolutions and are persuaded that we have the will to do wonders. . . .

What would happen if we never committed those faults which make us love our humble state? We should think we were saints! ∾

> St. Jane de Chantal
> *Her Exhortations,*
> *Conferences and Instructions*

AT PEACE WITH IMPERFECTION

This rule is general: No one will be so holy in this life as not to be always subject to committing some imperfection or other.

We must keep ourselves constant and tranquil in the knowledge of this truth if we will not be troubled with the unrealistic expectation of never committing any imperfection at all. We should have a strong and constant resolution never to be so cowardly as to commit any imperfection voluntarily. But we ought also to be unshaken in this other resolution: not to be astonished or troubled at seeing that we are subject to fall into these imperfections, even often. We must rather confide ourselves to the goodness of God who, for all that, does not love us less. "But I shall never be capable of receiving the divine caresses of our Lord while I am so imperfect; I shall not be able to approach him who is so sovereignly perfect." What relation, I pray you, can there be between our perfection and his, between our purity and his, since he is purity itself? In short, let us for our part do what we can and remain in peace about the rest.

We find those who hope for nothing so much as to be Mother Teresa [of Avila] very soon, and even Saints Catherine of Siena and Genoa. That is good; but tell me, how long do you give yourself for this task? "Three months," you reply, "even less, if it is possible." You do well to add, "if it is possible," for otherwise you would be much deceived. Do not those fine hopes, notwithstanding their vanity, greatly console those who have them? But the more these hopes and expectations bring joy to the heart, while there is reason for hope, so much more does the contrary condition bring sadness to those fervent souls. Not finding themselves the saints they had hoped to be, but, on the contrary, very imperfect creatures, they are very often discouraged in the pursuit of the real virtue which leads to sanctity. "Gently," we say to them. "Do not hurry so fast! Begin to live well, according to your vocation: sweetly, simply, and humbly. Then trust in God, who will make you holy when it pleases him." ∾

St. Francis de Sales
Sermons for Lent

CLOTHE YOURSELF WITH GOD'S PERFECTION

Go forward joyfully and don't check to see whether you have insight, understanding, and similar gifts. Be content that our Lord is rich in all these gifts and graces. Love them in him, and don't desire them at all for yourself. Blessed are the poor in spirit. What great riches we possess when we desire nothing but God! In this is our happiness. . . .

Won't you, then, make this full and irrevocable surrender of yourself into God's hands? Strip yourself of all self-concern and desire for virtue, wanting no virtues but those that God will give you—according to the opportunities that come up and to which you must respond faithfully. Naked and without virtue I came into the world, and without any virtue whatsoever do I commend myself into your hands, my God. Say this, my daughter, and whenever you see that your spirit wants to clothe itself once again, having stripped itself of everything, do nothing except to simply bring it back to its God. And remain in the arms of his providence like a child, leaving all your concerns unreservedly to God.

For your spiritual distress comes only from the fact that you don't have the perfection you want. But you must be content with the perfection our Lord wants you to have, since real perfection lies in this resignation and tranquility of spirit. . . . If your work isn't followed by success, embrace these crosses lovingly, and rejoice at your lack of joy. Blessed are the naked, for God will clothe them. May his Goodness give us the grace to be completely stripped. ❧

St. Jane de Chantal
Correspondance

The Purpose of Pain

From a letter to an abbess undergoing great physical pain:

W hat do you think a bed of suffering is? It is nothing else than the school of humility where we learn all about our misery and weakness, and how vain, delicate, and weak we are. And so, beloved daughter, it is on that bed that you will discover your imperfections. Why there, I ask, more than elsewhere, save that anywhere else they remain hidden within the soul, whereas in suffering, they become visible. The turbulence of the sea affects every type of person, even those who think themselves quite well, for, after sailing a while, they discover, through the seasickness brought on by the violent tossing of the waves, that they are not as invulnerable as they thought. One of the great benefits of suffering is that we come to see the depths of our own nothingness, and that the debris of our bad inclinations floats to the top. But are we to be disturbed on that account, dear daughter? Certainly not. It is then that we have to cleanse and purify our heart still more, and take greater advantage than ever of the sacrament of confession. . . .

Self-love . . . is one of the sources of our disturbance; the other is the importance we give ourselves. Why is it that when we happen to commit some imperfection or sin, we are so surprised, upset, and impatient? Without doubt, it is because we thought we were something special, resolute, and steady, and therefore, when we discover that in reality we are nothing of the kind and have fallen flat on our face, we are disappointed, and consequently we are vexed, offended, and upset. If we really knew ourselves well, instead of being astonished at finding ourselves on the ground, we would marvel that we ever manage to remain standing up. That's the other source of our disquiet: we want nothing but consolation and are taken aback when we see and experience our misery, our nothingness, and our weakness. ❧

St. Francis de Sales
Letters of Spiritual Direction

9

Little Things

IN THE VALLEY
OF THE LITTLE VIRTUES

From a letter to a young woman in a religious community:

Our Lady's Son was born in the stable. Courage, then: let us prepare a place for this holy infant. Our Lady loves only places that are made low by humility, common by simplicity, but large by charity. She is willingly near the crib and at the foot of the cross. She doesn't mind if she goes into Egypt, far from all comfort, provided she has her dear Son with her. . . .

Let us advance, then, let us advance. Let us make our way through these low valleys of the humble and little virtues. We shall see in them the roses amid the thorns, charity which shows its beauty among suffering; the lilies of purity, the violets of death to self. What won't we see!

Above all, I love these three little virtues—gentleness of heart, poverty of spirit, and simplicity of life—and also these concrete practices: visiting the sick, serving the poor, comforting the afflicted, and the like. All of this, though, without overeagerness but with true liberty of spirit.

No, our arms aren't yet long enough to reach the cedars of Lebanon. Let's content ourselves with the hyssop of the valleys. ❧

St. Francis de Sales
Letters to Persons in the World

GREAT LOVE TRANSFORMS SMALL DEEDS

There are people who imagine doing great things for God, things that would involve great suffering and heroic actions. Yet there is no opportunity to perform such deeds—and perhaps there never will be. They believe that just by imagining these deeds, they have shown great love, but they are often deceived. For while they desire to embrace great future crosses, they anxiously avoid the much lighter burdens that are presented to them now. Isn't it a big temptation to be heroic in imagination, but cowardly in carrying it out?

God, preserve us from these imaginary fervors, which so often produce a vain and secret pride in the bottom of our hearts! Great works do not always come our way, but in every moment, we may do little ones well—that is, with a great love. Look at that saint, I ask you, who gives a cup of cold water to a thirsty traveler. He does only a small deed outwardly, but the intention, the kindness, the love which inspires him is so wonderful that it turns this simple cup of water into the water of life, and of eternal life.

The bees gather honey from the lily, the iris, and the rose, yet they get as much honey from the minute rosemary flowers and thyme. In fact, they draw not only more honey, but even better honey from these, for in these small vessels the honey is more concentrated and better preserved. It is true: in the little works of devotion, love is not only practiced more frequently but usually more humbly as well, and consequently more usefully and productively.

Putting up with other people's moods and troublesome behavior, gaining victory over our own moods and passions, renouncing our petty preferences, coming against our own revulsions, honestly acknowledging our faults, keeping our souls in peace, loving our lowliness, gently and graciously welcoming scorn or criticism of our way of life, of our conversation, and of our actions—Theotimus, all these things are more beneficial to our souls than we can imagine, if we let God use them for this purpose. ❧

St. Francis de Sales
Treatise on the Love of God

SEEING GOD IN THE ORDINARY

From a letter to a married woman:

Respond to the occasions for dying to yourself that come up most often, for this is the first thing we must do; after that we will do others. In spirit you should often kiss the crosses which our Lord has himself placed on your shoulders. Do not check to see whether they are made of precious or fragrant wood. They are truer crosses when they are made of vile, lowly, worthless wood. It is remarkable that this always comes back to my mind and that I know only this song. Without a doubt, my dear sister, it is the canticle of the Lamb; it is somewhat sad, but it is harmonious and beautiful: "My Father, let it be done not as I will, but as you will" (cf. Matthew 26:39).

Mary Magdalene seeks our Lord though she already has him; she asks for him and it is him she asks. She is not content to see him as he is and seeks to find him looking otherwise. She wanted to see him in his glorious robe, not in a gardener's lowly attire. Still, at last, she knew it was the Lord when he said, "Mary" (cf. John 20:16).

See here, my dear sister and daughter: it is our Lord in gardener's dress that you meet here and there every day when ordinary occasions of dying to yourself come your way. You would like him to offer you other and finer-looking mortifications. But the finest-looking ones are not the best! Don't you think that our Lord is saying "Mary,

Mary?" to you? No, before you see him in his glory he wishes to plant many flowers in your garden; they are little and lowly, but they are the kind he likes. That is why he comes to you dressed the way he is. ∾

St. Francis de Sales
Letters to Persons in the World

THE LITTLE WAY TO GREATNESS

From a talk to the nuns in her care:

In my opinion, if you use well the opportunities that come your way of dying to yourself and practicing virtue, you will do quite as much and more for your perfection [than if you were to undertake strenuous ascetic practices]. . . . Rest assured that if you accept in all humility and simplicity whatever is presented to you—regarding things like food and clothing and also the mortifications, humiliations, and contradictions you receive—that will be as good as the austerities you practice or desire to practice, and even much better. For what dying to self is there in things when you have chosen them? You don't find those very difficult; you take pleasure in them and feel complacent about them. Doesn't our saintly father [Francis de Sales] say plainly enough, "Our own choice spoils all our works"? . . .

Be very faithful about responding to occasions for putting virtues into practice. For instance, is there something about your clothing or your bed that inconveniences and annoys you—something that doesn't fit well or that isn't to your liking? Accept it heartily, kiss it, if you can, and be very glad to have it. Perhaps the soup given to you at dinner is too thin or too thick; or it is unsalted or watery; there is not enough oil on your salad or the vinegar is not strong enough. Rejoice at these opportunities to discipline your sense of taste. Embrace them with love and cheerfulness. . . . Something you don't like is given to you; something has been forgotten, but you can do without it—love all situations like this. Adapt yourself to God's providence, which allows them. If you know how to take them in the right way, you can benefit by them and grow in the perfection of divine love. ❧

St. Jane de Chantal
Her Exhortations,
Conferences and Instructions

DON'T SEEK THE LOFTY HEIGHTS

There are certain things which many consider as virtues but are not such at all. I must say a word about them: these are ecstasies or raptures, experiences of insensibility, impassability, deific unions, levitations, transformations and other such perfections treated in some books. They promise to raise the soul to purely intellectual contemplation, to a total concentration of the spirit and to a supereminent life. You see, Philothea, such perfections are not virtues. Rather they are rewards which God gives for virtues. Better still, they are a fore-taste of the happiness of the life to come given sometimes to men to make them long for its fullness in paradise. But for all that we must not seek such graces since they are in no way necessary for serving and loving God well, who ought to be our sole aim.

Often these are not graces which can be acquired by one's own effort and skill since they are more passive than active. We can receive them but not create them in us. I add that we have only undertaken to make our-selves good persons, persons committed to devotion, devout men and women. Therefore we must work hard for it. If it pleases God to elevate us to such angelic per-fection, we shall be also good angels.

While awaiting, let us simply, humbly and devoutly exercise ourselves in small virtues, the conquest of which Our Lord has entrusted to our care and toil: such as patience, good-naturedness, mortifications of the heart, humility, obedience, poverty, chastity, tenderness towards our neighbor, bearing their imperfections, dili-gence and holy fervor.

Let us willingly leave lofty heights to the exalted. We do not deserve such a high rank in the service of God. We shall be extremely happy to serve him in his kitchen, in his pantry, to be his servants, porters or attendants. Later, if it pleases him, it is for him to take us into his Cabinet and Privy Council. Yes, Philothea, this King of

Glory does not reward his servants according to the dignity of their office but according to the love and humility with which they carry them out. . . .

While blessing God for the supereminence of others, let us be firm on our way: lower but safer, less excellent but more suited to our insufficiency and littleness. If we continue in it, humbly and faithfully, God will raise us to great heights which are great indeed. ❧

St. Francis de Sales
Introduction to the Devout Life

Step by Tiny, Imperceptible Step

In prayer, union with God takes place through small but frequent movements of the heart: "Yes, Lord, I am all yours—all, all, without any exceptions! I am most assuredly yours, Lord, and I want to be increasingly yours! Dear Jesus, draw me ever forward into your heart so that I may be engulfed in your love and know the depths of your kindness!". . .

The human heart uproots itself from worldly concerns and roots itself in God through heavenly love if it strenuously engages in prayer. Then, certainly, our hearts will keep on expanding and will embrace Divinity, becoming more and more united with God's goodness. But this growth is imperceptible. We don't easily notice its progress either as it unfolds or once it has been accomplished.

How blessed is the person who, in tranquility of heart, lovingly maintains the sacred sense of God's presence! For this person's union with divine Goodness will continue growing perpetually, though imperceptibly, and will fill her whole spirit with its infinite sweetness. . . . ❦

St. Jane de Chantal
Sa Vie et ses oeuvres

LITTLE TEMPTATIONS

Wolves and bears are obviously more dangerous than flies, but they are less annoying and do not try our patience so much. It is easy to refrain from murder, but it is difficult to refrain from little outbursts of anger for which opportunities arise at every moment. It is easy for a man or a woman to refrain from adultery but it is not easy to refrain from amorous glances, from giving or receiving flirtatious love, from soliciting little favors, from speaking or listening to words of flattery. It is easy to admit of no rival to the husband or wife as far as the body is concerned, but it is not easy to do so with regard to the heart. It is easy not to be unfaithful to one another in married love, but hard to refrain from everything that may be injurious to it. It is very easy not to steal the goods of others, but difficult to refrain from envy and covetousness. It is very easy not to bear false witness in a court of law but difficult not to tell lies in conversation. It is easy not to wish the death of another, but difficult never to wish him harm. It is easy never to slander a man, but difficult never to despise him.

In short, little temptations to anger, suspicion, jealousy, envy, flirtation, vanity, frivolity, duplicity, affectation, deceit, unchaste thoughts—these are the trials which even the most devout and resolute must constantly face. Therefore, Philothea, we have to prepare ourselves for this battle with great care and diligence. Be sure that, for all our victories over these little enemies, as many precious stones will be set in the crown of glory which God prepares for us in heaven. Because of this, I repeat, while being ready to fight courageously against great temptations when they come, we must defend ourselves well and diligently against these little and feeble assaults. ∾

St. Francis de Sales
Introduction to the Devout Life

COMMON SENSE FOR TRAVELERS TO HEAVEN

From a letter to an abbess undergoing great physical pain:

Let us go by land, since the high sea makes our head spin and makes us seasick. Let us stay at our Lord's feet, like Mary Magdalene (cf. Luke 10:39) whose feast we are celebrating. Let us practice those little virtues that are appropriate for our littleness. Little peddler, little pack.

These are the virtues which are practiced more in going downhill than in going up, so they suit our legs better: patience, bearing with our neighbor, submissiveness, humility, sweetness of temper, good-naturedness, tolerance of our imperfections, and other little virtues like these. I do not say that we are not to climb up by prayer, but that we should do so step by step.

I recommend to you holy simplicity. Focus on what is in front of you and not on those far-off dangers you see. . . . To you they look like armies, but they are only willow branches, and while you are looking at them you may take a false step. Let us have a firm basic intention to serve God all our life and with all our heart. Beyond that, *let us have no anxiety about tomorrow* (cf. Matthew 6:34). Let us think only of doing well today. When tomorrow arrives, it will in turn become today and we can think about it then. Here again we must have great confidence and acceptance of God's providence. We must provide ourselves with only enough manna for each day (cf. Exodus 16:16-21). And we must not doubt that God will rain down more manna on us tomorrow, and the day after tomorrow, and all the days of our pilgrimage. ❧

St. Francis de Sales
Letters to Persons in the World

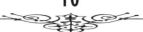

10

Love God, Love Neighbor

From a talk to the nuns of her religious community:

God is to be loved above everything else, and after him our neighbor. . . . This is the way of all perfection. If we keep this commandment well, all the rest will be very easy for us. For in this one, said our Lord, lie the law, the prophets, and the perfection of true Christians: to love God with our whole heart, our whole strength, our whole understanding, our whole mind and soul, and our neighbor as ourselves (cf. Matthew 22:37-40).

I suspect that we hardly think enough about the weightiness of this commandment. Do we ever apply our heart, thoughts, strength, understanding, and soul to nothing but loving God? Indeed, our frailty is so great that sometimes we prefer our little preferences, wills, and petty fancies to the purity of love of God and of right reason.

And do we ever do to our neighbor nothing but what we could wish done to us? Are we as pleased at her welfare as at our own? Do we truly hide her faults? Are we indeed responsive to all her wishes? Do we have a sense of her sorrows? Are we very careful to console, serve, and comfort her? Oh, no, no! We usually want to be preferred to our neighbor. And nevertheless, you see what this commandment obliges us to do. This is why I urge you from the bottom of my heart to give it careful and serious attention.

You know that for us, our nearest neighbors are our dear sisters with whom we live. I urge you, therefore, to this union of hearts and mutual love of one another so that you may worthily receive the blessings which God has always willingly poured out on communities that are united with one mind in his love. ❧

> St. Jane de Chantal
> *Her Exhortations,*
> *Conferences, and Instructions*

WHY SHOULD I LOVE MY NEIGHBOR?

The charity that produces acts of love for God produces, at the same time, acts of love for our neighbor. And even as Jacob saw a single ladder touching heaven and earth, so that the angels could go both down and up (cf. Genesis 28:12), we know that the same charity extends to both the love of God and our neighbor. It raises us to the union of our spirit with God, and brings us back again into a loving relationship with our neighbors. However, this is always on the understanding that we love our neighbor as being created in the image and likeness of God, made to communicate with the divine, to participate in his grace, and to enjoy his glory. . . .

Ah, then, Theotimus, when we see a neighbor who is created in the image and likeness of God, shouldn't we say, "Look and see how this person resembles the Creator?" Shouldn't we embrace him, caress him, and weep over him with love? Shouldn't we bless him a thousand times over? And why? For the love of him? Not really: for we don't know whether he is worthy of love or hatred in himself (cf. Ecclesiastes 9:1). But why then? O Theotimus! For the love of God, who made him in his own image and likeness, so that he is capable of participating in his goodness, in grace and in glory. For the love of God, I say, from whom he is, whose he is, by whom he is, in whom he is, for whom he is, and whom he resembles in a most intimate way. Thus, the love of God not only often commands the love of our neighbor, but it also produces this love and pours it into our hearts, as its own image and likeness. For even as man is made in the image of God, so the sacred love of man towards man is the true image of the heavenly love of man towards God.

St. Francis de Sales
Treatise on the Love of God

"As I Have Loved You"

From a talk to the nuns in her religious congregation:

B y the grace of God, we don't hate our sisters passionately or wish them any evil. But this isn't enough: we must love one another from the heart. . . . We must respect our sisters and want all sorts of good and prosperity for them. We must desire their perfection and progress in the love of God as much we desire our own. It isn't enough not to trouble and annoy them: we must assure their peace of heart, their consolation and joy. In short, we must do them all the good we can. . . .

Our Lord told us that we should love as he loved us. He said to his disciples, "By this all men will know that you are my disciples, if you have love for one another" (John 13:35). . . . Certainly, we can never reach the perfection of this holy love and union with God unless we have this love of neighbor. Yesterday, I was reading what St. John wrote: "If anyone says, 'I love God,' yet hates his brother, he is a liar; for he who does not love his brother, whom he sees, cannot love God whom he does not see" (1 John 4:20). If we don't have heartfelt love and holy affection towards our sisters, who represent God's image to us, we must conclude that we don't have true love of God. . . .

Let us see if we're harboring any slight bitterness of heart toward any of our sisters—any jealousy, ambition, dislike. . . . Before God, let's examine ourselves to see if we desire the good of all our sisters equally, one as much as another. To speak very gently with those for whom we feel a special attraction and liking, to say nothing that downgrades them, to do nothing that puts them out—these are not the marks of perfect charity. Real charity and true virtue require that we speak to all our sisters in the same way—gently, cordially, with humble frankness, sweet confidence, holy joy and gladness, and with a good word about all. . . . It is in this that virtue lies, not in our own preferences. And if we happen to find some sisters disagreeable or hostile toward us, we must remember this: "Do good to those who hate you. Bless those who persecute you; bless and do not curse them" (Luke 6:27; Romans 12:14).

Let's all examine our hearts . . . and if we find in ourselves any resentment, aversion, or remembrance of past wrongs, let's immediately pick up the pruning hook of God's holy fear and cut off this evil shoot. . . . In its place, let's build up love for this great commandment towards our neighbor and for following this holy precept to "love one another as I have loved you" (John 13:34). ❧

St. Jane de Chantal
Her Exhortations,
Conferences and Instructions

SINS OF SPEECH ARE SINS AGAINST LOVE

From a talk to the nuns in her care:

It's very easy to sin against our neighbor with our tongue. This is why Scripture says: "He who guards his tongue preserves his soul" (Proverbs 13:3). . . . We sin against our neighbor—or rather God in our neighbor—when we speak inappropriately and also sometimes by being silent. Suppose that when I'm told something good about a person for whom I have no great love, someone who has displeased me, I hold my tongue or answer coldly. By this I offend God, . . . for I'm making it known that I don't think much of that person. Perhaps my coldness will destroy the good opinion others had. . . . Or say I answer with some secret little diminishing words; like a drop of oil that falls on cloth and widens out, these will impress themselves indelibly in the heart of the person to whom I'm speaking. And note well that whatever evil is done because of the bad impression I've communicated will be on my own conscience. . . .

How subtle self-love is! . . . If we liked the person in question or felt obligated or in sympathy with her or hoped to receive something from her, we'd find a thousand good things to say about her virtues without scrutinizing their truthfulness for fear of lying. But people we don't associate with or feel a liking towards leave us dry, and then we dry up the hearts of others.

Often, though, there are more virtues to recount about those we pass over than those we praise.

We behave as we do because we live according to the spirit of the world and our own understanding. But the spirit of reason and the grace of God would have us make known the good which God has placed in his creatures, without consulting our own preferences. We displease and offend God by concealing and diminishing the good in our neighbor. . . . And when we don't know anything about the virtue for which someone is being praised, we must not keep silent on that account but skillfully say something good. . . . However disagreeable a person may be, we can always find something good to say. ❧

St. Jane de Chantal
*Her Instructions,
Conferences and Exhortations*

HOLY AND SACRED FRIENDSHIP

Love everyone with a great love of charity but have friendship with those capable of communicating virtuous things to you. The more exquisite the virtue you put in your exchanges the more perfect will your friendship be. If you share knowledge, your friendship is indeed very praiseworthy; more so, if you communicate virtues, prudence, discretion, fortitude and justice. If your mutual and reciprocal exchange is about charity, devotion, Christian perfection, precious indeed will your friendship be. It will be excellent because it comes from God, excellent because it tends to God, excellent because its bond is God, excellent because it will last eternally in God. How good it is to love on earth as one loves in heaven, and to learn to cherish one another in this world as we shall do eternally in the next! . . .

Perhaps many people may tell you that you should not have any kind of special affection and friendship since it occupies the heart, distracts the mind and creates jealousies. But they err in their advice. . . .

It is necessary that those who live among worldly people and embrace true devotion join together in a holy and sacred friendship. By this means they encourage, assist and support themselves well. Just as those who walk on level ground do not need a helping hand, but those who are on a dangerous and slippery path support one another to walk more safely, so too those who are religious do not need particular friendships.

But those who are in the world do need them, to save themselves and help one another, in the midst of so many difficult paths they have to cross. In the world, all do not strive for the same end, all do not have the same spirit. Hence, without doubt, it is necessary to draw oneself aside and form friendships according to our aim. This particularity is indeed a partiality but a holy partiality, which does not cause any division except between good and evil, between sheep and goats, and between bees and hornets—a necessary separation. ❧

St. Francis de Sales
Introduction to the Devout Life

SERVING OTHERS WITH DEVOTION

The ways by which we can unite ourselves to our neighbor are very numerous; but I will mention only a few of them. Since God wants us to love and cherish others, we must see our neighbor in him. This is the counsel of St. Paul who orders servants to serve God in their masters and their masters in God (cf. Ephesians 6:5-7). We must practice this love of our neighbor and express it outwardly; and even if at first we seem to do so reluctantly, we must not give up on that account, for this feeling of aversion will, in the end, be conquered by the habit and good dispositions that result from repeated acts. We must bring this intention to our prayer and meditation; having begged God for his love, we must ask him also to grant us love of others, especially of those persons we have no inclination to love.

I advise you to take the trouble now and then to visit hospitals, to comfort the sick, and to have compassion for their infirmities, letting these touch your heart; and pray for the sick even as you give them whatever help you can. But in all this, be very careful that your husband, your servants, and your relatives be not inconvenienced by overly long visits to church, by too lengthy withdrawals to pray and noticeable neglect of your household responsibilities or, as sometimes happens, by your trying to control the actions of others, or showing too much disdain for gatherings where the rules of devotion are not precisely observed. In all these instances charity must prevail and enlighten us so that we yield to the wishes of our neighbor in whatever is not contrary to the commandments of God.

You must not only be devout and love devotion, but you must render it lovable to everyone. Now you will make it lovable if you render it useful and pleasing. The sick will love your devotion if they receive care and comfort from it; your family will love it if they see you more attentive to their well-being, more gentle in handling affairs, more kind in correcting, and so on; your husband will love it if he sees that as your devotion increases, you become more warm and affectionate toward him; your relatives and friends will love it if they see you more free, supportive of others, and yielding to them in matters that are not contrary to God's will. In short, we must, as far as possible, make our devotion attractive. ∞

St. Francis de Sales
Letters of Spiritual Direction

LOVE DOES THESE THINGS

From Jane de Chantal's testimony in Francis de Sales' canonization process:

In all the nineteen years that I had the happiness of knowing him well, both before and after I became a nun, I never knew him to fail to do for his neighbor all the good that lay within his power. He never spared himself in this service; I am quite sure of this, and have seen and experienced more of it than I can ever tell you. . . .

He once wrote to me: "When shall we be really steeped in a sweet and tender love for our neighbor? When shall we really see his soul in our Savior? Alas, if we look at him in any other way, we run the risk of not loving him purely, faithfully and each one alike. But who could help loving him in our Lord, putting up with him and bearing his faults? Who could then find him unattractive or tiresome? For that's where our neighbor really is, right in our divine Savior's heart, so beloved and so lovable that the Lover dies for love of him.". . .

Everybody knows that he never turned anyone away, however miserable a sinner he might be. He often gave large alms to fallen women so as to help them lead a good life; and when some of them sinned again and then turned to him once more, he received them with the same kindness. When his servants pointed out to him that this was a waste of time and money, he answered that it was indeed a sad state of affairs, but that as long as there was any hope of converting a sinner we had to help him. . . .

He had in the highest possible degree a loving and universal care for everything to do with his neighbor's want, and he made no exceptions. Those who were always with him can bear special witness to this unremitting service.

He never turned anyone away. Whatever the time, however important the business that was waiting for him, he hardly ever dismissed anyone who came to see him, nor did he show any signs of weariness or aversion. And when people remonstrated with him for being so easy of access that it made him waste time, as they pointed out, on unimportant people and negligible causes, he answered gently: "You call these little people unimportant, but they need to be listened to just as much as the great. . . . They come to be comforted, so why shouldn't we give them all the comfort we can?". . .

He helped people financially though his own means were limited. . . . Twice a week, on Mondays and Thursdays, there was a general distribution of alms at his house, quite apart from daily almsgiving; and if there was a hard season he arranged for an increase. . . .

He often gave away his outer clothes, his linen and his shoes; once, as his valet assured me, he even handed out the shoes he was wearing. . . . The year after he died two Jesuit fathers told me that they had met the village schoolmaster of Faucigny who showed them a vest which the Blessed had given him one winter when he was too poor to buy warm clothes. He asked him if he had nothing warmer to wear than what he had on, and when the other said no, the Blessed went into his little inner room, took off his woolen vest, put on the rest of his clothes again and handed him the garment in a discreet way.

St. Jane de Chantal
A Testimony

11

Live Jesus!

DEVOTION THAT SPRINGS FROM THE HEART

Those who deal with rural agricultural matters assure us that, if some word is written on an almond seed that is quite entire, and put back in its shell carefully, and properly folded and closed, and thus planted, then every fruit which the tree produces will have the same word written and engraved on it. As for myself, Philothea, I could never approve the method of those who begin by the exterior such as the bearing, the dress or the hair in order to reform a man. On the contrary, it seems to me that we should begin by the interior: Convert yourself to me, says God, with your whole heart (Joel 2:12). My child, give me your heart (Proverbs 23:26). As the heart is the source of actions, they are such as the heart is. The divine Spouse inviting us says: Place me as a seal on your heart, as a seal on your arm (Song of Songs 8:6). Yes, indeed, anyone who has Jesus Christ in his heart, will have him soon after in all his exterior actions.

I wish, therefore, dear Philothea, to engrave and inscribe on your heart, before everything else, this holy and sacred maxim: LIVE JESUS! After that, I am sure that your life which comes from your heart, like the almond tree from its kernel, will produce all its actions which are its fruits inscribed and engraved with the same word of salvation. Just as this gentle Jesus will live in your heart, he will live also in your conduct and appear in your eyes, in your mouth, in your hands, even in your hair. Then you could say reverently following St. Paul, I live now, not I, but Christ lives in me (Galatians 2:20). In short, he who has won the heart of man, has won the whole man. ∿

St. Francis de Sales
Introduction to the Devout Life

To Find Yourself, Lose Yourself in God

To be lost in God is nothing else than to be absolutely and wholly resigned and given over into God's hands . . . . These words "to be lost in God" have a certain meaning which I think can be understood only by those who are happily lost. The great St. Paul understood it well when he said with such assurance, "It is no longer

I who live, but it is Christ who lives in me" (Galatians 2:20). How happy we would be if we could truly say this! To live no more in oneself but lost in God is the most sublime perfection the soul can reach. We should all aim for this, losing ourselves again and again a thousand times in the ocean of this infinite greatness. . . .

Now, some of us want to lose ourselves, but we also want it not to hurt too much. We do indeed tell our Lord that we're surrendering ourselves into his divine arms, but we don't do it in the right way. We want to retain some degree of control—not so much in temporal matters as in spiritual ones; self-love, with its subtle tricks, always tries to persuade us that things won't go the way they should unless we remain somewhat involved in them. But people who are completely lost in God don't want to have any virtue or perfection except what God wants. They work faithfully, because God wishes it, but they let God take concern for their work. They don't go looking for new methods of achieving perfection but simply concentrate on making good use of the ones that providence supplies and offers in every situation.

It's true that even once we've given ourselves to God completely, we tend to take back the gift. What else is there to do, in that case, but humble ourselves, acknowledge the incompleteness of our surrender, . . . and follow this act of deep humility by . . . throwing ourselves back into God like a little drop of water falling into the sea—losing ourselves in the ocean of the divine Goodness, never to find ourselves again. Repeat this process constantly, and if you faithfully persevere in it, I dare promise you that you will lose yourself at last and never find yourself again. Such a happy loss!...

How true these words are: "If we have died with Christ, we believe that we will also live with him" (Romans 6:8). It is our great St. Paul who says them. Let us believe him, and we will see he speaks the truth. ∾

St. Jane de Chantal
Her Exhortations,
Conferences and Instructions

LIVING IN THE SPIRIT

To live according to the spirit is to think, speak, and act according to the virtues that are in the spirit, and not according to the senses and feelings that are in the flesh. We must use and subject the latter and not live according to them, but the spiritual virtues must be followed and given dominion over all the rest. . . .

To live according to the spirit is to love according to the spirit; to live according to the flesh is to love according to the flesh, for love is the life of the soul as the soul is the life of the body. One person is very sweet, very agreeable, and I love him tenderly. He loves and favors me greatly, and I love him in return. Who wouldn't see that I'm living according to the senses and the flesh? For even animals, who are without a spirit and have only flesh and senses, love their benefactors and those who are kind and pleasant with them. Another person is uncouth, sharp-tongued, and ill-mannered; all the same, she is very pious and wants to improve herself and learn to be more sociable. I love her, I go to her, I serve her, I embrace her—not because I find her pleasant or hope to get something out of it, but to please God. This love is according to the spirit, for the flesh has no share in it.

I distrust myself and for this reason would rather be left alone so that I could live according to that desire. Who could fail to see that this is not living according to the spirit? . . . When I was quite young and had no understanding yet, this is how I lived. But although I am timid and fearful by temperament, I still want to try and overcome these natural tendencies and, little by little, learn to do properly everything that is part of the office that obedience, coming from God, requires of me. Who could fail to see that this is living according to the spirit?

Living according to the spirit is to do the actions, say the words, and think the thoughts which the Spirit of God requires of us. ∽

St. Francis de Sales
Letters to Persons in Religion

HOLY SPIRIT, HAVE YOUR WAY WITH ME

T he great method for mental prayer is simply this: that there is none when the Holy Spirit has taken charge of the person who is meditating, for then he does with the soul as it pleases him, and all rules and methods vanish away. In the hands of God the soul must become like clay in the hands of a potter, who from it can form any sort of dish; or, if you like, the soul must become like soft wax receptive to the impression of a seal, or like a blank sheet upon which the Holy Spirit writes his divine will. If, when entering upon prayer, we could make ourselves a mere capacity for receiving the spirit of God, this would suffice for all method. Prayer must be carried on by grace, and not by deliberate art. Enter into your prayer by faith, remain in it in hope, and do not abandon it except by virtue of that charity which asks only to work and to endure.

The fundamental state of mind for mental prayer is that purity of intention by which we are resolved that everything we do shall be for the glory of God alone. The second condition is a complete self-resignation which may make us indifferent to anything that can happen to us. The third is a complete giving up of our own opinions so that we labor only at that which God has given us for our labor.

St. Jane de Chantal
St. Chantal on Prayer

HUNGRY FOR GOD

From a letter to Jane de Chantal:

You tell me that you feel more than usually starved for Holy Communion. . . . Humble yourself as much as you can, my daughter, and warm yourself inside with the holy love of Christ crucified, so that you can spiritually digest this heavenly food as you should. . . .

But what do you think this means, digesting Jesus Christ spiritually? People who have a good digestion feel their whole body strengthened as the food distributes itself evenly to every part of them. In the same way, my daughter, people who have a good spiritual digestion feel that Jesus Christ who is their food penetrates to every part of their soul and of their body and communicates himself to them. They have Jesus Christ in their head, heart, breast, eyes, hands, tongue, ears, and feet. But what does our Savior do in them? He straightens every-thing out, purifying, mortifying, quickening all things. He loves in our heart, understands in our head, inspires our actions within us, he sees in our eyes, he speaks with our tongue, and so with all the rest: he does everything in us, and then we live, not we ourselves, but Jesus Christ lives in us. O when will that be, my dear daugh-ter? When, O God? But in the meanwhile I am show-ing you what to aim for even though we must be content to get there gradually. Let us stay humble and go to Communion trustfully; little by little our faculty of spiritual digestion will get accustomed to this food and will learn to assimilate it as it should. . . . If we only long for our Savior, then I have every hope that our digestion will be good. ❧

> St. Francis de Sales
> *Selected Letters*

THE NAME ABOVE ALL OTHER NAMES

I'm under such pressure that I don't have time to write you anything more than the great word of our salvation: JESUS.

If only we could say this sacred name from our hearts just for once! Oh, what sweet balm it would spread to all the powers of our spirit! How happy we should be to have only Jesus in our understanding, only Jesus in our imagination. Jesus would be everywhere in us, and we would be everywhere in him.

Let us try this; let us pronounce this sacred name as often as we can. And if for the present we can only stammer it, in the end we shall be able to say it properly.

But how should that sacred name be pronounced? . . . Alas, I don't know. I only know that to speak it appropriately, we need a tongue all of fire. That is, it takes nothing less than divine love, which is the only thing capable of expressing Jesus in our lives by impressing him in the depths of our heart. But courage! Surely, we will love God, for he loves us. Rejoice in this and don't let your soul be troubled about anything. ❧

St. Francis de Sales
Letters to Persons in Religion

Sources and Acknowledgments

*The editor and publisher wish to express their
gratitude to Sister Peronne Marie Thibert, V.H.M.,
for graciously making available the resources of
Visitation Monastery library in
Mendota Heights, Minn., and to the following for
permission to reproduce material:*

Introduction to the Devout Life by St. Francis de Sales.
Translated and edited by Armind Nazareth, M.S.F.S.,
Antony Mookenthottam, M.S.F.S., Antony
Kolencherry, M.S.F.S. Malleswaram. © 1990 by S.F.S.
Publications, Bangalore, India.

St. Francis de Sales. Selected Letters.
Translated by Elisabeth Stopp. © 1960 by Elisabeth

Stopp. Published by Faber & Faber, London and Harper and Brothers, New York. Used by permission of the literary executor of Elisabeth Stopp.

The Sermons of St. Francis de Sales. Vol. 1: On Prayer. Translated by Nuns of the Visitation [Frances Therese Leary], edited by Lewis S. Fiorelli, O.S.F.S. © 1985 by TAN Books and Publishers, Rockford, Ill. Used by permission of TAN Books and Publishers.

The Sermons of St. Francis de Sales. Vol. 3: Lent. Translated by Nuns of the Visitation [Frances Therese Leary], edited by Lewis S. Fiorelli, O.S.F.S. © 1987 by TAN Books and Publishers, Rockford, Ill. Used by permission of TAN Books and Publishers.

St. Chantal on Prayer. Translated by Rev. A. Durand. © 1968 by Daughters of St. Paul. Used by permission of Pauline Books and Media, 50 St. Paul's Ave., Boston, Mass. All rights reserved.

St. Francis de Sales: A Testimony by St. Chantal. Translated by Elisabeth Stopp. © 1967 by Elisabeth Stopp. Published by Institute of Salesian Studies, Hyattsville, Md., and Faber & Faber, London. Used by permission of the literary executor of Elisabeth Stopp.

Francis de Sales and Jane de Chantal: Letters of Spiritual Direction. Translated by Peronne Marie Thibert, V.H.M. © 1988 by Peronne Marie Thibert, V.H. M., Wendy M. Wright, and Joseph F. Power, O.S.F.S. Used by permission of Paulist Press, Mahwah, N.J.

Two excerpts have been freely translated by the editor from the following French sources:

Sainte Jeanne de Chantal, Correspondance, édition critique établie et annotée par S. Marie-Patricia Burns, vsm. T. 6, "Lettre 2615." Editions du Cerf, Paris, 1996.

Sainte Jeanne-Françoise Frémyot de Chantal, Sa Vie et ses oeuvres. T. 3, Conseils de direction, "Divers degrés d'oraison." Plon, Paris, 1876.

All other excerpts have been taken, often adapted and paraphrased, from the following:

Treatise on the Love of God, by St. Francis de Sales. Translated by H. B. Mackey, O.S.B. The Newman Bookshop, Westminster, Md., 1942.

Library of St. Francis de Sales. Translated and edited by H.B. Mackey, O.S.B. Burns & Oates/Burns, Oates, & Washbourne, London,

1873-1910. Vol. 1: *Letters to Persons in the World;* Vol. 4: *Letters to Persons in Religion;* Vol. 5: *Spiritual Conferences.*

Selected Letters of St. Jane Frances de Chantal. Translated by the Sisters of the Visitation, Harrow-on-the-Hill. Washbourne & Oates, London, 1918.

The Spirit of Saint Jane Frances de Chantal as Shown by Her Letters. Translated by the Sister of the Visitation, Harrow-on-the-Hill. Longmans, Green, and Co., London, 1922.

St. Jane Frances Frémyot de Chantal: Her Exhortations, Conferences and Instructions. Translated by the Sisters of the Visitation, Bristol, England, from the French edition printed at Paris in 1875. The Newman Bookshop, Westminster, Md., 1947.

For Further Reading

*Francis de Sales: Finding God Wherever You Are.
Selected Spiritual Writings.* Introduced and edited by
Joseph F. Power, O.S.F.S. New City Press, New York,
1993.

Francis de Sales, Sage and Saint, by André Ravier.
Translated by Joseph D. Bowler. Ignatius Press, San
Francisco, 1988.

*Bond of Perfection: Jeanne de Chantal and François de
Sales,* by Wendy M. Wright. Paulist Press, New York,
1985.

Thy Will Be Done: Letters to Persons in the World, by
St. Francis de Sales. Sophia Institute Press,
Manchester, N.H., 1995.

See also the introduction to *Letters of Spiritual
Direction,* as well as *St. Francis de Sales, A Testimony
by St. Chantal,* mentioned above.

Other Resources from The Word Among Us Press

Also available from the Wisdom Series:
My Heart Speaks, Wisdom from Pope John XXIII
Meet this warmhearted, saintly man through selections from his personal journal, letters to his family, speeches and encyclicals.

Welcoming the New Millennium, Wisdom from Pope John Paul II
A collection of some of the Holy Father's most inspiring writings, on subjects ranging from prayer and forgiveness to evangelism and marriage.

Walking with the Father, Wisdom from Brother Lawrence
Learn from this seventeenth-century Carmelite brother how to abide in God's presence no matter what you are doing or how busy you are.

Touching the Risen Christ, Wisdom from the Fathers
The writings from the early Church Fathers become more accessible to the contemporary reader in this collection of sermons in an easy-to-read translation.

From the Gospel Devotional Commentary Series:
Matthew: A Devotional Commentary
Mark: A Devotional Commentary
Luke: A Devotional Commentary
John: A Devotional Commentary
Leo Zanchettin, General Editor

Enjoy praying through the gospels with commentaries that include each passage of scripture with a faith-filled meditation.

Books on the Saints:
A Great Cloud of Witnesses: The Stories of 16 Saints and Christian Heroes by Leo Zanchettin and Patricia Mitchell

I Have Called You by Name: The Stories of 16 Saints and Christian Heroes by Patricia Mitchell

Each book contains inspiring biographies, along with selections of the saints' own writings.

To order call 1-800-775-9673
www.wau.org